BRUCE WEBER'S
★ INSIDE ★
PRO FOOTBALL

◇ 1985 ◇

SCHOLASTIC INC.
New York Toronto London Auckland Sydney

ISBN 0-590-33839-0

12 11 10 9 8 7 6 5 4 3 2 1   9   5 6 7 8 9/8 0/9

CONTENTS

With All-Pro quarterback Dan Marino again at the controls, the Miami Dolphins hope to win Super Bowl XX.

INTRODUCTION:
The Road to Super Bowl XX

The 1985 season is, at least in part, the Year of the College Quarterback. First, it was Boston College's Doug Flutie. He signed with the USFL's New Jersey Generals and made plenty of noise on the publicity front. But Flutie was one of the few real stars of the college ranks signed by the new league after the '84 NCAA season. After two years of grabbing some of the better available talent, the USFL's near shutout on the signing front may spell the beginning of the end for the spring (and maybe fall) league.

Then there was Bernie Kosar. The quarterback, who led the U. of Miami to the 1983 national college title as a freshman, decided that two years of college football was more than enough. (Unlike other collegians who left early, Kosar was ready to receive his degree.) The race for Kosar involved the Vikings, Oilers, Browns, and Bills — and Pete Rozelle. Rozelle gave Kosar a choice in the NFL draft, which triggered joy in some quarters and despair in others.

But 1985 promises to be even more. In a weird year, when Billy Martin got his umpteenth shot at managing baseball's New York Yankees, pro football looks at a year when dozens of teams are looking to see if 1984 was the real thing. Are the 49ers really the best team in the game, or did coach Bill Walsh do it with mirrors and a great short passing game? Was Miami's Dan Marino as good as his regular-season numbers, or can he be rattled, as San Francisco proved in Super Bowl XIX?

Are the Seattle Seahawks, who impressed everyone by going 12–4 after losing star runner Curt Warner only minutes into the season, ready to take over in the AFC West? Can the Chicago Bears get enough out of their quarterback position to utilize the game's best talent and secure a date in New Orleans next January?

For the have-nots, there are questions, too. Can the Philadelphia Eagles forget their front-office squabbles and return to the NFC East race? Is there anyone playing with a full deck in the front office of the New Orleans Saints?

There are high expectations in places where no one really knows what to expect. Include both New York teams in that class, along with Detroit, Green Bay, Kansas City, and a couple of others. Can new coaches really make a difference for Tampa Bay or Indianapolis? And what can a new-old coach do about erasing terrible memories in Minnesota?

All in all, 1985 should be an interesting and important year for the NFL. With new TV contracts coming up for negotiation, will the public, at home and at the ballpark, show the kind of interest that TV networks translate into dollars?

It should be fun. Stay tuned.

— Bruce Weber

National Football League All-Pro Team

Wide Receiver
ART MONK
WASHINGTON REDSKINS

The Washington Redskins' patience has finally paid off. When they drafted Art Monk of Syracuse in the first round of the 1980 draft, they believed they had a new superstar to go with some of the great receivers in Skins' history. After several years of growing up and recovering from injuries, Monk is right there — along with Bobby Mitchell, Charley Taylor, and Jerry Smith — Redskin legends all.

Redskin coach Joe Gibbs, who isn't exactly overgenerous with praise, said of Art's 1984 season: "Art made the most valuable contribution I've ever seen by a wide receiver to his team." Not bad. Neither was the season. Art's 106 catches were five more than the all-time pro record of 101, set 20 years ago. He was the NFL's Offensive Player of the Week *twice*. In the closing seconds of the final game, which the Redskins needed to make the play-offs, Art snuck between two Cardinals to set up the winning field goal.

A national champion high school hurdler and an All-American at Syracuse, Monk had never missed a game until a 1983 injury put him on the sidelines for a month. But the man is quick, durable, solid, and a sure-fire All-Pro.

Wide Receiver
ROY
GREEN
ST. LOUIS CARDINALS

Roy Green is one of those rare athletes who can do anything well. Everyone knows how the Cards took an outstanding young defensive back and converted him into one of the NFL's best deep receivers. But did you also know that Roy played nearly every position at Magnolia (Arkansas) High School? If only his coaches could have cloned Green, who saw action at quarterback, wide receiver, tight end, running back, cornerback, and safety. He probably could have played major league baseball, and he was a natural in track. A one-man athletic department was young Roy.

Still, it was football that finally brought him fame, and, eventually, fortune. It took three years for Roy to really make his mark with the Cards, competing for a job at strong safety. Then, during 1981, he took advantage of an opportunity to help out at wide receiver. It took a year or so, but Roy finally found his place, and he hasn't been stopped yet.

Now, at age 27, Roy has added a new dimension to the Cards. Last season the numbers read 78 catches and 1,555 yards, the third-highest yardage total in league history. He averaged 19.9 yards per catch and had 12 TD catches, the NFC's best.

Offensive Tackle
JOE
JACOBY
WASHINGTON REDSKINS

For those nonfans who think that Boss Hog is a character out of *The Dukes of Hazzard*, don't hang around Washington. In the capital, Redskin freaks know that THE Boss Hog is Joe Jacoby, the leader of the Skins' offensive line (the Hogs).

Ask Washington strength coach Dan Riley who the strongest Redskin is, and he'll tell you that the contest is for second place. None of the Skins comes close to Jacoby. Jake, as Jacoby is called by friends, is also quicker than your average tackle. On the Skins' famous Counter Trey play, Jacoby pulls out along with guard Russ Grimm, making it awfully tough on Washington opponents.

The highlight of 1984 for Jacoby (and perhaps his entire career) was his touchdown against Minnesota. Viking defensive back Keith Griffin fumbled into the end zone. Jacoby pounced on the ball for the first TD ever by a Washington offensive lineman. He leaped to his feet and spiked the ball so hard that it will forever be remembered as the "Jake Quake."

At 6–7 and 300 pounds, Jacoby casts a mighty shadow, whether he's blocking for the run or protecting QB Joe Theismann. The one-time free agent could be an All-Pro for years.

Offensive Tackle
KEITH FAHNHORST
SAN FRANCISCO 49ERS

It took 11 seasons, but everyone now knows that San Francisco's Keith Fahnhorst has stepped to the head of the class of NFL offensive tackles. The Super Bowl champ 49ers' super right tackle allows opposing pass rushers to sack QB Joe Montana about as often as you get an A on a test you didn't study for.

While we don't know about your study habits, we do know that Fahnhorst allowed his first sack of 1984 in the Niners' eleventh game. The former U. of Minnesota tight end seems to have gotten better every year. He was really upset in '83 when he wasn't chosen to the NFC Pro Bowl team. So he went out and had an even better season in '84 — and won every honor he could.

At 6–6 and 273, the 33-year-old has great size and quickness for an NFL tackle. He is wonderfully durable also. When he missed a game with the Steelers last October, it marked his first absence after 90 straight starts.

Keith has lots of fans, including his brother Jim, a San Francisco linebacker. But one of his biggest rooters is Niner coach Bill Walsh. "Keith is at the peak of his career," says Walsh. "He must be one of the very best tackles in the league."

7

Offensive Guard
ED NEWMAN
MIAMI DOLPHINS

For years, Miami's press department made headlines with the No-Name Defense, the Killer B's, and, now, Dan Marino. What about the no-name offense? It starts with Ed Newman, one of the finest offensive linemen in the game and a household word — in his own household!

Big Ed (6–2, 255), twice an ACC wrestling champion at Duke, sat for the better part of six seasons before becoming the Dolphin starter in 1979. Since then he hasn't missed a game or a start, earning Pro Bowl honors in each of the last four seasons.

Thanks to Marino, the Dolphin offensive line has begun to get the recognition it deserves. By leading the league in fewest sacks allowed for the last two seasons, the Dolphin inside group has shown everyone what AFC coaches have known for years.

Newman is clearly one of the most popular Dolphins. He was the Dolphins' choice for their entry in the NFL Man of the Year contest. Ed does a lot to help various charities in the Miami area. Opposing tackles only wish he was as charitable with them.

Newman remains as one of the game's most talented and inspirational players. His recovery from cancer in 1975 earned him tremendous respect and admiration.

Offensive Guard
JOHN HANNAH
NEW ENGLAND PATRIOTS

When Raymond Berry took over the New England coaching post midway through the '84 season, he admitted that he didn't know much of the club's personnel.

That did not include John Hannah, of course. The All-Pro guard has been the rock of the Pats' offensive line since 1973. They're already staking out a spot for him at the Pro Football Hall of Fame.

Son of one NFL tackle and brother of another (the Raiders' Charley), John didn't have his best season last year. Fact is, by Hannah standards it may have been only an average year. But Hannah standards are so high that there isn't a guard in the league who wouldn't settle for an average Hannah year.

Ask John and he may tell you that the highlight of his career was the touchdown he scored on a fumble recovery back in 1974. Ask any other Pat and you'll find out that their highlight is watching big (6–3, 265) John work on blowing holes in opposing defenses.

There was plenty of confusion in New England a year ago — switching offenses, players, and coaches. With more stability in '85, and a healthy Hannah, things should improve.

DWIGHT STEPHENSON
MIAMI DOLPHINS

The folks in Miami knew it years ago. The folks around the AFC found out about it a couple of seasons back. Now everyone in the NFL knows — that Dwight Stephenson has become the league's No. 1 center.

It seemed in the past that a center had to be around for at least 10 years before he could be considered the league's top snapper. Remember Jim Otto with the Raiders and Mike Webster with the Steelers? After only five years with the Dolphins, Stephenson has reached that top level.

Statistics usually separate the runners, receivers, and throwers. And statistics can also tell the tale for linemen. Miami allowed the fewest sacks in the NFL last year (14). In fact, 1984 was the second straight year that the Dolphins took this honor. According to Miami coach Don Shula, Dwight Stephenson deserves a major share of the credit.

The 6–2, 255-pounder from Alabama has been the AFC's Pro Bowl starter for three straight years, after a college career that saw his coach, Bear Bryant, call him "the greatest center I've ever coached." The "center of attention" on Miami's offensive front does wonders for Dan Marino and his mates.

Quarterback
DAN MARINO
MIAMI DOLPHINS

Super Bowl XIX or not, Dan Marino is our choice for All-Pro quarterback of 1985. You might well add 1986, 1987, and a couple of years beginning with 199, too.

There isn't a football player (or fan) who wouldn't trade everything for a piece of Dan Marino's future. Overlooked early in the 1983 NFL draft, Marino became the most amazing of coach Don Shula's many amazing draft picks by becoming a solid starter as a rookie and then breaking every single-season passing record in the book as a sophomore.

A lot of great quarterbacks put in hundreds of great years (combined) without ever matching Dan's 1984 show: 48 TDs (old record: 36); 5,084 yards (old record: 4,722); four 400-yard games; nine 300-yard games; 362 completions. Wow!

"There were times last year when I wanted to jump up and give the guy a standing ovation," says Shula. "Nobody has ever had a year like that for me, and I've coached some pretty fair quarterbacks in my day."

Critics point to Miami's horrid Super Bowl showing and give receivers Mark Duper and Mark Clayton much credit for Marino's success. But Marino's fans have only one question: What can he do for an encore?

11

Running Back
WALTER PAYTON
CHICAGO BEARS

In all the hoopla before the '84 season, everyone guessed how long it would take Franco Harris to overtake Jim Brown's running record. Brown bellowed, Harris fumed . . . and then it was over. Spurned by the Pittsburgh Steelers, Franco signed with the Seattle Seahawks, and lasted just a few weeks.

Meanwhile, one of the NFL's most popular stars, Chicago's Sweetness, Walter Payton, quietly passed both Franco Harris and Jim Brown — and shows no sign of slowing down.

For years, Payton was just about the entire Bears' team. They played decent, hard-sticking defense. But the offense was just about "zippo." Now, especially when QB Jim McMahon is healthy, Walter gets plenty of help — and a few victories, too.

At age 30, Payton has two more years on his current Bear contract. He'll probably sign another multiyear pact, too. When he passed Brown's 12,312-yard mark, he kept right on going. His current goal is 15,000 yards, which he could reach in 1986.

"You have to have goals," says Payton. "That's what keeps you going. When you lose your desire, that's the time to hang it all up."

Running Back
ERIC DICKERSON
LOS ANGELES RAMS

The way the fans see it in southern California, Walter Payton is going to keep hold of the all-time rushing records only until Eric Dickerson is ready to take permanent possession.

The fans may have a point. With the single-season record (formerly held by O.J. Simpson) now safely tucked away in his Rams' equipment bag, Dickerson takes off for new worlds to conquer. Clearly they aren't worlds designed for normal football players.

The 6–3, 218-pounder was the second player picked in the 1983 NFL draft. (Denver QB John Elway was the first.) The former SMU star adjusted to the NFL and the Rams' one-back offense quickly, setting high standards as a rookie and then shifting into even higher gear as a sophomore. The afternoon he broke Juice's 2,003-yard record, he ran for 215 yards. Just another routine "day at the office" for Dickerson, who wears glasses on the field.

Overall, Eric gained 2,105 yards on 379 carries last year, a 5.6-yard-per-carry average. He also gained 100 yards or more in 12 games, another all-time record. If the man stays healthy, he'll own all of the records before he's done.

13

Tight End
OZZIE NEWSOME
CLEVELAND BROWNS

About the only uprising in Cleveland last year was the scream for coach Sam Rutigliano's scalp. That, it turned out, didn't help. But Browns' fans had some good things to cheer about, especially their all-time leading receiver, tight end Ozzie Smith.

The 6–2, 232-pounder enters his eighth NFL season as a marked man. With a limited offense, the Browns often turn to the 29-year-old Alabama grad. He broke four Browns' receiving records last season, and he added to four others. Check out these numbers: 440 career catches and 5,570 career yards, 89 catches in a season (in each of the last two years), and 14 catches and 191 yards in one game (against the Jets in '84).

The departed Rutigliano loved his super tight end. "No one in the league goes after the ball like Ozzie," said Rutigliano. "If we get the ball close, he'll get it. It doesn't matter if they're pushing and shoving. Ozzie's too tough."

Want to stop Newsome? Call the Redskins and ask for the films of their October 24, 1979, game against Cleveland. The 'Skins' defense must have figured out something. That's the last time anyone has shut out tough Ozzie.

14

Defensive Line
MARK GASTINEAU
NEW YORK JETS

The Jets' Mark Gastineau does everything big. He plays big (6–5, 270 pounds); he lives big (including a $150,000 Rolls Royce); he helps big (making all sorts of donations to children's charities); he's big at the bank (earning nearly $750,000 a season).

Jet opponents need no introduction to No. 99. Offensive game plans are often geared to blunting the charge of the speedy (4.6 in the 40), quick, huge Gastineau. Double- and triple-teaming are ways of life for Mark, who is still the key to the Jets' Sack Attack. "Boy," says Gastineau, "would I love to go one-on-one with the offensive tackles in this league." It'll never happen.

Jet coaches worry about Gastineau's health. Many teams assign blockers to cut his legs out from the blind side, which, if not illegal, is certainly dangerous. But that doesn't seem to stop the seven-year star. About the only way to stop Mark is through a rule change — like the one that halted his "sack dances."

Gastineau isn't the most popular player around, particularly among Jet opponents. Still, when Kansas City quarterback Bill Kenny calls him simply "the best defensive end in football," that's praise enough.

Defensive Line
LEE ROY SELMON
TAMPA BAY BUCCANEERS

Many NFL offensive coaches throw out half of their rushing playbooks when they get ready to play Tampa Bay. The reason: To run at outside linebacker Hugh Green and defensive end Lee Roy Selmon isn't overly wise. Your blockers won't be thrilled, and your runner may question your wisdom.

Rumor has it that certain left-handed-hitting baseball players try any excuse to keep from hitting against some left-handed pitchers. The same is true for offensive left tackles who are scheduled to meet up with Mr. Selmon.

An All-American at Oklahoma, Lee Roy (king of the football-playing Selmon brothers) quickly became the No. 1 Buc. At 6–3 and 245 pounds, he isn't as big as most DEs in the NFL. (For example, Mark Gastineau is 6–5 and 270.) Still, he possesses super quickness and great strength. At age 30, he knows the value of staying in shape, which he does with joy — and with his family — during the off-season.

"Even if I have lost a step or two," says Selmon, "I've more than made up for it with experience." It may well prove valuable enough for Lee Roy to become the Bucs' first Hall-of-Famer. Buc fans hope, of course, that it won't be soon.

Defensive Line
RANDY WHITE
DALLAS COWBOYS

When the "Manster" — half man, half monster — failed to show up in Dallas' training camp last summer, panic set in. Better coach Tom Landry pass up the season than Randy White. Everyone was sure Randy would show up. Well, pretty sure.

After some extended breath-holding, the 6-4, 263-pounder finally did appear — in time to start every Cowboy game and to prove that he's one of the greatest defensive tackles ever.

When All-Pro pickers go to work, they generally start with the ex-Maryland star. He's made the All-Pro group seven straight years, an all-time Dallas record. He racks up important numbers like a bingo-caller. He led the defensive line in tackles — again; he led the team in sacks — again; and he was the team's defensive MVP in five straight victories.

The Manster's durability might lead a lot of players to sit out training camp. Randy has played in 147 straight regular-season games, starting 76 of them. Although he didn't practice until August 27, he played every down on defense in 1984.

Though the Cowboys once projected Randy as a linebacker (he failed there), he turned out to be a pretty decent DT.

Defensive Line
HOWIE
LONG
LOS ANGELES RAIDERS

A friend of ours, Dick Corbin, is the line coach at Harvard University. Before that, however, he was an outstanding high school coach in Massachusetts — thanks, in some measure, to coaching players like Howie Long.

Actually, there aren't many players like Howie Long, and Corbin has the stories to prove it. Long, at 6–5 and 270 pounds, is one of the NFL's toughest hombres, a title he has carried from his high school days.

In only his fourth pro season, Howie is an All-Pro for the second straight year and went to the Pro Bowl for the second time. Why not? He's close to vicious on the field, finishing second among the Raiders in sacks (11 in 17 games, including one in the play-offs) and making 58 tackles.

His great size makes him a troublemaker just about anywhere on the field. He's especially good at knocking down passes (just in case he can't knock down the quarterback). Statistically, 1984 was his best season.

Howie combines super strength and outstanding mobility, the keys to success for any NFL defensive lineman. And add versatility, too. Howie does equally well at tackle or end.

Linebacker
LAWRENCE TAYLOR
NEW YORK GIANTS

By making the play-offs (and even winning one postseason game), the Jersey Giants pulled off the Minor Miracle of the Meadowlands. Which means that Lawrence Taylor enjoyed his usual beyond-belief season, but this time some of his teammates chipped in, too.

L.T., as the fans lovingly call the best defensive player in the game, is a one-man wrecking crew. He pops up all over the Giant "D," and he's a threat from any spot. Offensive coaches have been known to suffer a sleepless week when their team is scheduled to face the Giants the next Sunday.

Raves one NFL quarterback — after an afternoon of wear and (mostly) tear, "Our entire game plan was designed to handle L.T. Forget it. He ruined us."

At 6–3 and 245 pounds, Taylor has become the model by which outside linebackers are judged. That's a remarkable achievement for someone who didn't play football until his junior year in high school. In fact, only two colleges went after L.T.

Since then, Taylor has put on a few pounds, added lots of muscle, and improved his speed to 4.5 for 40 yards. It's his quickness, as much as his strength, that makes him the best — perhaps ever.

19

Linebacker
MIKE SINGLETARY
CHICAGO BEARS

Watch out, Dick Butkus. For years, when you said middle linebacker in Chicago, everyone automatically shouted, "Dick Butkus." Now Butkus is making commercials and nursing a pair of chewed-up knees. But Mike Singletary is doing his share in making long-suffering Bear backers forget King Dick.

Chicago made its living on defense a year ago (what a collection of quarterbacks!), and Singletary, the ex-Baylor star, was right in the middle of it. Easily the most improved LB in the league, Mike has proven to his coaches that he can now defense the pass as well as the run. It was a major weakness in his game when he arrived, mainly because he wasn't asked to do it in college. Now he's one of the best; he's a complete player.

"When they kept taking me out in passing situations," remembers Mike, "I was getting a message. I wanted to be in there all the time, but the coaches knew I wasn't ready. Fact is, early on I must have looked like a clown on pass coverage. Playing full-time tells me something, too. I've reached part of my goal — becoming a complete player." Bear defensive boss Buddy Ryan puts it even better: "Mike's super!"

Linebacker
CLAY MATTHEWS
CLEVELAND BROWNS

There wasn't much to write home about in Cleveland last year. The Browns reached a low point when coach Sam Rutigliano was asked to leave at midyear. But there was plenty of excitement in at least one area: the Linebacking Division of the Defense Department.

Tom Cousineau and Chip Banks get plenty of ink — and they deserve it. But the guy who made things happen is Clay Matthews. Not a giant at 6–2 and 235 pounds, right outside 'backer Matthews is on the verge of becoming Cleveland's all-time best pass-rusher.

Ask Steve Bartkowski of the Falcons. Big Bart was sacked 10 times by the Browns (who won 23–7) last season, with 3½ sacks credited to Matthews (who gives the impression that he's a madman on the loose). The last sack ended with Bartkowski being carted off the field.

Browns' coach Marty Schottenheimer, starting his first full season at the helm, compares Matthews to the Steelers' all-timer, Jack Ham, at a similar time in his career. That's a big reputation to live up to. But Clay knows that when he plays well, his teammates do, too. That's enough motivation.

Cornerback
LOUIS WRIGHT
DENVER BRONCOS

All those football players who think pre-season training is overrated will now point in the direction of Louis Wright. The Broncos' 32-year-old left cornerback missed all of the '84 preseason with a pulled thigh muscle. Then the season began, and Louis zipped off another in a long line of All-Pro seasons.

Wright, a first-round Bronc draft choice (from San Jose State) in 1975, is the leader of an outstanding Denver defensive backfield. The five-time Pro Bowler sets an amazing example for right corner Mike Harden and safeties Steve Foley and Dennis Smith.

Denver assistant coach Charlie West marvels at Louis: "We put him out there, ask him to take his guy man-to-man, and help the other backs, too. It's quite a challenge, but Louis always responds." There's a statistic the Broncos use to prove the point: opponent TDs by beating Louis Wright — 0. None. Zero. Zip. What a season for a veteran player who still owns most of the speed that made him a champion sprinter and long jumper in college.

The 6–2, 200-pounder is at an age when many NFL cornerbacks are retired. Louis has shown no reason to even think about it.

Cornerback
MIKE HAYNES
LOS ANGELES RAIDERS

It looks as if the Raiders will have to do some patching to make a run at Super Bowl XX this winter. But one position they don't have to worry about is right cornerback. Ten-year-vet Mike Haynes has that neatly wrapped up, playing the position better than anyone else in the game.

Raider rivals pay their respects to the one-time New England Patriot in an unusual way: They simply don't throw the ball in his direction. (Not that left corner Lester Hayes is much easier!) When enemy aerials do come his way, Mike knows what to do. Quarterback Dan Marino of the Dolphins, who owned the airwaves in '84, tried and failed to dent Haynes' armor. Haynes picked off Marino twice, returning one 97 yards for a score and the other 54 yards to set up another touchdown.

"I like the Raiders' attitude," says Haynes, an outstanding all-round athlete. "We don't have to win pretty. We just have to win. We can give up 50 points, so long as we score 51. Al Davis says it best. 'Just win, baby.' That's terrific."

Haynes' ability to force opponents to throw away from him means that his stats aren't too fancy. But his performance is, and that's what counts.

MICHAEL DOWNS

DALLAS COWBOYS

In a year of distress in Dallas, Mike Downs stood out. He led the Cowboys in tackles, which doesn't say much for the team's defense. Free safeties simply should not lead a team in tackles.

Still, Michael did what he had to do — and gets the nod for an All-Pro safety spot over Chicago's Todd Bell and San Francisco's Dwight Hicks.

It took four seasons for Downs to become an NFL star. Michael became a starter in his first game in 1981. But when he came to camp in '84, he wasn't sure of anything. Personnel chief Gil Brandt told Downs that he hadn't played very well in '83. Michael thought that he'd have to play more aggressively, which was out of character for him.

Whatever it was, it worked. The 6–3, 205-pounder became a terror, especially when a safety blitz was in order. He also intercepted seven passes and tied for second in the NFC in that department.

He may have played his best game on national TV — with no one watching. In a late-starting game against New Orleans, Dallas was way behind and TVs clicked off — before Downs' two intercepts and one fumble recovery turned things around.

KEN EASLEY
SEATTLE SEAHAWKS

We remember watching Kenny Easley early in his college career at UCLA. "Easily" was a better name for the easy way the young man played this tough game. Our opinion has never wavered, and now every expert in the game agrees.

Blessed with great athletic ability and given great freedom in the Seattle defensive plan, Easley is the key to the Seahawks' amazing turnover ratio. Seattle had 63 take-aways last year, which is a plus-24 over their turnover number. The Hawks' ability to take advantage of enemy mistakes made them one of the league's most feared teams.

Easley, one of the hardest-hitting backs in the NFL, had 83 tackles last season, fourth highest on the team — highly unusual for a safety. But Kenny is unusual. He also had a league-leading total of 10 interceptions, and returned two of them for scores. He also forced three fumbles.

Just so Ken didn't waste his spare time, he also returned punts for Seattle last year, when starter Paul Johns was hurt and went on injured reserve. "I knew someone had to help," he says easily. Even there, he finished third in the AFC with a 12.1-yards-per-return average.

25

All-Pro Clay Matthews is a key to the Browns' chances of getting back in the AFC Central race.

American Football Conference Team Previews

AFC East
MIAMI DOLPHINS
1984 Finish: First
1985 Prediction: First

Kim Bokamper   **Tony Nathan**

The major question for the Dolphins in '85
is: Can Miami bounce back from its Blow-
out Sunday in Palo Alto last January?

The answer here is yes! There's simply too
much talent — and too much coach Don
Shula — for us to believe anything else. Not
that there aren't some personnel problems
to solve along the Road to Super Bowl XX.
It's just that Shula always seems to come up
with the right answers.

There's no question at QB, where Dan
Marino is likely to write his own chapter in
the record book before he's through. He
tends to force passes at times, but with his
arm, he gets away with them — most of the
time.

The running game, on the other hand,
needs a boost, particularly from a quick,

outside threat. The returnees include reliable receiver Tony Nathan, dependable Woody Bennett, injury-prone Joe Carter, and overstuffed Pete Johnson.

But there's plenty of receiver speed, with Mark "Super" Duper, Mark Clayton, Nat Moore, and Jimmy Cefalo. TE Joe Rose is a fine receiver. It's a great bunch.

The offensive line is easily the AFC's best, led by All-Pros C Dwight Stephenson and RG Ed Newman. LG Roy Foster is improving his pass-blocking, a skill already mastered by LT Jon Geisler. Eric Laakso may return at RT after a spell on injured reserve.

More help is needed on defense. The line is satisfactory, particularly nose man Bob Baumhawer, who plays the position as well as anyone. Bob is the leader of the Killer B's, along with ends Doug Betters on the left and Kim Bokamper on the right. Both are tough to throw against, though Bokamper needs help on the run.

Linebacking is far more questionable. Inside men A.J. Duhe and Earnest Rhone have suffered crippling injuries, with Duhe probably finished. Youngsters such as Mark Brown, Jay Brophy, and Jackie Shipp will likely get full shots. On the outside, both Bob Brudzinski and Charles Bowser are first-rate.

A healthy Don McNeal at cornerback will help shore up the backfield, with CB William Judson, and brothers Glenn and Lyle Blackwood at safeties.

AFC East
NEW YORK JETS
1984 Finish: Third
1985 Prediction: Second

Marvin Powell   **Lance Mehl**

Only the most loyal Jet fans remember that the team was 6–2, nearing the midpoint of the '84 season. The rest of the campaign was a disaster that is best forgotten by all concerned.

Coach Joe Walton begins the new year with an entirely new defensive coaching staff, but with some question marks on the field. Still, there are enough talented players for the Jets to turn it around now.

After a season-long game of "Who's the Quarterback?" Kenny O'Brien should get the nod over Pat Ryan. Both showed flashes of stardom a year ago, but neither seems to be a Super Bowl quarterback.

Likewise, the running game is okay, when Freeman McNeil is healthy. Injuries limited McNeil to 1,070 yards last year, a great total for most but only fair for McNeil. Johnny Hector is an excellent partner.

Up front there's plenty of strength with C Joe Fields, RT Marvin Powell, and RG Dan Alexander. The left side of the line leaves something to be desired. G Jim Sweeney should develop.

The receiver corps depends on the health of Lam Jones and Wesley Walker, with Walker the subject of trade rumors. Top draft choice Al Toon should fit in.

The new defensive staff needs a pass-rusher and a middle linebacker to get things going again. Defensive coordinator Bud Carson will switch to a 3–4 set, adding to the linebacker pressure. All-Pro end Mark Gastineau has provided most of the Jets' pass-rush recently, especially with Joe Klecko hampered by on-going injuries. Young Ron Faurot and vet Marty Lyons should help.

Several youngsters made fine first impressions last year, providing future hope. Both Kyle Clifton and Bobby Bell saw plenty of action, along with vets Lance Mehl and Greg Buttle. Good drafting and good health will help.

In the secondary, there's the lovely question of where to play last year's rookie star, Russell Carter. Other vets, such as Darrol Ray and Ken Schroy, are in trouble.

If Walton can patch up his relationship with some of his players and his soft spots on the field, the Jets could come back strong in '85.

AFC East
NEW ENGLAND PATRIOTS
1984 Finish: Second
1985 Prediction: Third

Ray Clayborn

Stanley Morgan

The honeymoon is over for coach Ray Berry. Patriot players were delighted when the all-time wide receiver replaced harsher Ron Meyer midway through the '84 campaign. They responded by splitting their final eight games, missing the play-offs they expected to make.

Now Berry starts fresh, with a mostly new coaching staff and some high expectations. He probably has a better shot than Meyer, mainly because the players like him and the team has solved its quarterbacking question with Tony Eason. After replacing Steve Grogan, Eason hit 60.1% of his passes and threw for 23 scores and 3,228 yards.

Look for a healthy Irving Fryar to help the passing game, where tight end Derrick

Ramsey set an all-time Pat record with 66 pass receptions (and seven TDs). There's plenty of depth at the wide position, though long-time star Stanley Morgan has begun to drop the ball on ordinary plays.

Aging John Hannah remains the game's best offensive guard at age 34. Pete Brock must bounce back from injuries at center, with T Brian Holloway, T Darryl Haley, and G Ron Wooten in decent shape.

Berry may switch back to a two-back offense from Meyer's one-back set. Craig James, over from the USFL, was a major '84 surprise, leading the Pats in rushing with 790 yards and a 4.9 per-carry average. There's plenty of depth, with Mosi Tatupu, Tony Collins, and Robert Weathers.

The defensive line must be tremendously improved to take the pressure off the rest of the Pats' defense. Ends Ken Sims and Toby Williams and nose man Dennis Owens didn't put enough pressure on the opposing quarterback.

Linebacking is excellent, led by Andre Tippett on the outside and Steve Nelson on the inside. Larry McGrew and Don Blackmon do an adequate job.

The backs just need the up-front help. Ray Clayborn, the right corner, is outstanding, and left corner Ernest Gibson and safeties Roland James and Rick Sanford can get the job done. Depth is required, however.

Ex-Eagle Tony Franklin showed why he was a star in Philly, hitting on 22 of 28 field-goal attempts.

AFC East
BUFFALO BILLS
1984 Finish: Fifth
1985 Prediction: Fourth

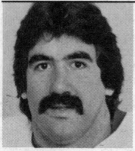

Fred Smerlas

Greg Bell

The best thing about the start of the '85 season for the Bills is that the '84 campaign is finally behind them. Though there were a few — very few — bright spots, last year ranks among the biggest disasters in football history.

Start with quarterback. Joe Ferguson was hurt through most of last year, and Joe Dufek couldn't do the job in relief. Matt Kofler and draftee Frank Reich each have a shot in '85.

The offensive line was tragic, with most of the same players who were among the best only a few years ago. Coach Kay Stephenson signed former line coach Jim Ringo to rebuild the front-line troops. Guard Justin Cross may return to tackle in '85, joining Joe Devlin and Ken Jones. Tom Lynch may push Jon Borchardt and former center Jim Ritcher at guard, with Will Grant the likely center. This group allowed 60 QB sacks (ouch!) in '84 and was called for holding 35 times! Mark Traynowicz will help.

Though the Bills were 27th in total offense, Greg Bell showed that he's ready to help for a long time. After gaining only 77 yards in his first four contests, he finished with 1,100, the 19th rookie in history to top 1,000. The rest of the bunch — Booker Moore, Van Williams, and Speedy Neal — isn't much.

Receivers such as Jerry Butler and tight end Tony Hunter must stay healthy, which they haven't in the past.

The defense, which actually improved throughout '84, looked bad because of the awful offense. ILB Eugene Marve was a marvel, leading the team in tackles with 188. Marve's inside partner, Jim Haslett, is excellent, with Darryl Talley and Lucius Sanford completing the foursome on the outside.

Up front, Outland Trophy winner Bruce Smith of Virginia Tech should improve a pass rush that recorded only 26 sacks. Injuries, particularly to end Jimmy Payne, hurt in '84. Nose man Fred Smerlas is outstanding, with ends Ken Johnson and Ben Williams trying for the spot opposite Smith.

Buffalo needs a left cornerback (rookie Derrick Burroughs?) to go with Charles Romes on the right side. Steve Freeman and Donald Wilson will likely get the call at the safeties.

AFC East
INDIANAPOLIS COLTS

1984 Finish: Fourth
1985 Prediction: Fifth

Vernon Maxwell   **Ron Solt**

New coach Rod Dowhower comes to the Colts with a reputation as a master of the passing game. But turning the Colts into a passing powerhouse will take all the skill Dowhower can muster.

The Colts' offense, which was murdered by injuries in '84, was totally toothless. They rotated the quarterback job between Mike Pagel, Art Schlicter, and Mark Herrmann, and none of the trio really did the job. In the final 11 games of the season, the Colts never scored more than 17 points, and their 239 total points were the lowest in the league.

The running game is fair when Curtis Dickey and Randy McMillan are healthy. Dickey, especially, wasn't in '84, and Frank Middleton couldn't do it.

The line, which lost several stars early, played hurt, especially LG Ben Utt. RG Ron Solt learned fast for a rookie.

The defensive medical list was as impressive as the offensive roster. ILB Cliff Odom played all year with a broken hand; NT Leo Wisniewski had knee problems; RCB Eugene Daniel suffered with leg ailments; CB James Burroughs missed half the season with an ankle problem.

Linebacking should be in fairly decent shape in '85, if everyone is healthy. RILB Barry Krauss and Odom were outstanding a year ago, as was LOLB Johnny Cooks. Watch rookie Duane Bickett.

Free safety Nesby Glasgow is the key man in a secondary that, by season's end, was playing rookies Preston Davis and Eugene Daniel at the corners.

Another rookie, Blaise Winter, was the starting right defensive end, opposite Donnell Thompson, who missed some playing time. There's some degree of hope up front.

Dowhower has plenty to do to get the Colts back into the AFC East title hunt. He got some bad news when Colt owner Robert Irsay, who spirited the Colts out of Baltimore under the cover of darkness a couple of years back, promised to take a more active role with the '85 Colts. With any kind of luck, the owner will realize that his place is in the office and the luxury box, not on the field and in the locker room. A wonderful wide receiver and an offensive line would help, too.

AFC Central
CINCINNATI BENGALS
1984 Finish: Second
1985 Prediction: First

Anthony Munoz   **Chris Collinsworth**

The Bengals are in the right place (the
weak AFC Central). But is this the right
time? Amazingly, 1984 almost was. Despite
an 8–8 record, Cincinnati missed the Central title (and play-off berth) by only one
game. Still, Cincy's record was probably not
a true indication of how poor the Bengals
were. And 1985 might not be much better.

There was some wonderful off-season
news, when star WR Cris Collinsworth (64
catches, 989 yards) was able to escape his
Tampa Bay (USFL) agreement. Having him
back should really help the Bengals.

Coach Sam Wyche has high hopes for '85,
after Cincy won eight of its last 11 in '84. His
coaching staff knows the players better, and
some of last year's youngsters have a year
of experience. Last year's first-round pick

Brian Blados is set at left guard, with third-round choice Stanford Jennings returning as the team's leading rusher (4.8 yards per carry) by average, the top kickoff returner (20.5 yards), and the No. 4 scorer. Second-year QB Boomer Esiason won a couple of games for Cincy as a rookie. Is Boomer ready to take over if Ken Anderson isn't ready for his 15th season? Stay tuned.

The defensive line (the Bengals play a 3–4) is in decent shape, with All-Star Ross Browner on the right and Eddie Edwards on the left. The linebackers are okay; and the secondary, led by corners Louis Breeden and Ray Horton and safeties Bobby Kemp and Robert Jackson, can do the job. The key is an improved pass-rush.

Offensively, Collinsworth is back, and Eddie Brown has arrived, easing the problem if Isaac Curtis retires. A healthy Anderson will solve the QB problems for another year. The runners, led by fullbacks Larry Kinnebrew (623 yards) and Charlie Alexander (479 yards) are not spectacular, but they work hard.

There's plenty of strength up front with mountainous Anthony Munoz set at left tackle, Blados at left guard, huge Dave Rimington at center, and Max Montoya and Mike Wilson on the right side.

The AFC Central figures to be most improved. (Why not? The quartet had the most improving to do.) Can the Bengals make the most improvement? With this bunch, anything is possible.

AFC Central
PITTSBURGH STEELERS
1984 Finish: First
1985 Prediction: Second

Rich Erenberg   Louis Lipps

Thanks in some measure to the pitiful AFC Central, the Steelers enter the '85 season as division champs, with their young players a year older — and, they hope, a year better.

Coach Chuck Noll will try to figure out what makes his club tick. The '84 team beat San Francisco (no one else did) and both Los Angeles teams. But six of their seven losses came against clubs with losing records. It's puzzling.

Big (6–4, 220) Mark Malone figures to get the start at QB, with ex-Dolphin David Woodley (who split the starts with Malone in '84). The Steeler running game was most improved last season, with Walter Abercrombie finally playing as everyone expected him to, and Rich Erenberg, a ninth-round pick, surprising everyone except himself. But the workhorse of the backfield is Frank Pollard, who seems to be banging someone on every play.

Steeler players voted John Stallworth as their most valuable teammate, after he bounced back to have his best year ever (80 catches, 1,395 yards). Exciting Louis Lipps (860 yards receiving, 656 yards on punt returns) took some pressure off Stallworth. Bennie Cunningham returns at tight end, where Darrell Nelson, Chris Kolodziejski, and John Rodgers also started last year.

Up front, Noll looks to youngsters Pete Rostosky and Craig Wolfley to start on the left side, along with center Mike Webster, the former All-Pro at center, and Terry Long and Tunch Ilkin on the right.

The defensive line must improve against the pass for the Steelers to really move up. John Goodman, Gary Dunn, and Edmund Nelson figure to start, with help from Keith Gary, Keith Willis, Mark Catano, and DeCarlos Cleveland.

The linebackers, led by brilliant LOLB Mike Merriweather, are the key to the defense. David Little, Robin Cole, and Bryan Hinkle figure to get the starting jobs.

More consistency is needed in the secondary, where the battle for starting positions and roster spots is the hottest. Safeties Eric Williams and Donnie Shell and corners Dwayne Woodruff and Sam Washington have the inside track, but a bunch of others are ready to take over.

AFC Central
HOUSTON OILERS
1984 Finish: Fourth
1985 Prediction: Third

Warren Moon   **Tim Smith**

Despite only three 1984 victories, the Oilers seem to be closing in on the rest of the AFC Central. That may be faint praise, but the Oilers could be making a big future for themselves.

QB Warren Moon, one year removed from football in Canada, has the Houston single-season passing record (3,338 yards) and a greater knowledge of the NFL.

Young guard Dean Steinkuhler and tackle Bruce Matthews man the right side of the offensive line with super Mike Munchak solidly set at left guard. They join Jim Romano (center) and Harvey Salem (left tackle) to provide Moon and friends with a sound, improving offensive line.

At age 28, Tim Smith has finally proven to be an outstanding wide receiver. He gets help from Mike Holston, who looks like a superstar — some of the time. Eric Mullins should get plenty of playing time.

Houston coach Hugh Campbell prefers the one-back offense, though his "one backs" aren't of championship quality. Larry Moriarty (785 yards) is a much improved receiver, while Stan Edwards works tremendously hard. Look for a healthy Willie Joyner and ex-Giant Butch Woolfolk to crack the lineup often. Both are quicker than the Moriarty-Edwards combo.

For the Oilers to really turn things around, they require a major overhaul on defense. Houston was among the league leaders in points allowed and rushing yardage allowed. Their success against the pass can be explained easily by their lack of success in stopping the ground game.

Houston needs help at defensive end for Bob Hamm and Jesse Baker. Mike Stensrud could return in the middle, though Brian Sochia could replace him. Rookie Ray Childress will start.

Among the linebackers, veterans Robert Brazile and Gregg Bingham could be gone (to the bench or from Houston) by opening day. Campbell is pleased with OLB Avon Riley and is convinced that inside man Robert Abraham could be a future star.

The secondary — corners Steve Brown and Willie Tullis and safeties Keith Bostic and Carter Hartwig — have had more practice making tackles than batting passes. They're okay.

AFC Central
CLEVELAND BROWNS
1984 Finish: Third
1985 Prediction: Fourth

Chip Banks   Joe DeLamielleure

Though the Browns are desperately trying
to forget 1984 — their 5–11 mark was the
third worst in Cleveland history — they
cannot forget that seven of the 11 losses were
by four points or fewer. Unfortunately, they
don't pay off on close in the NFL, and this
season may well be worse.

Coach Marty Schottenheimer, who replaced Sam Rutigliano midway through '84,
has a decent defense that can and should
get better and an offense that simply cannot make the big play.

The linebacking corps is one of the NFL's
best. With Chip Banks and Clay Matthews
on the outside and Tom Cousineau and
Eddie Johnson on the inside, the Browns
possess great strength.

Nor are the linebackers out there alone.

Nose tackle Bob Golic is also outstanding, playing between ends such as Reggie Camp and Keith Baldwin. There is hope in the secondary where cornerbacks Hanford Dixon and Frank Minnifield are up there with the best, and safeties Don Rogers and Al Gross hit hard.

The offense, on the other hand, needs lots of work. Schottenheimer spent the off-season figuring out what to do with the quarterback position, including the possibility of signing U. of Miami's Bernie Kosar, after trading Paul McDonald and picking up Gary Danielson.

The offensive line, which was hurt by the loss of tackle Cody Risien last year and Doug Dieken this year, is dangerously old and quite ineffective. G Joe DeLamielleure is 34, and G Robert Jackson is 32. The Medicare years.

There is some hope. TE Ozzie Newsome, the AFC leader with 89 receptions, is the best in the game. Youngsters such as wide receivers Brian Brennan and Bruce Davis, running back Earnest Byner, and defensive back Chris Rockins seem ready to jump in and help.

Meanwhile, running back Mike Pruitt has seen better days; and Boyce Green, the leading rusher, won't help win championships.

Prospects were bright in Cleveland only one year ago. Now it seems that the Browns are years away from mounting a real threat — even in the weak AFC Central.

AFC West
SEATTLE SEAHAWKS
1984 Finish: Second
1985 Prediction: First

Joe Nash   Steve Largent

When super RB Curt Warner went down
for the season 11 minutes into the 1984 campaign, things looked awfully bleak for the
Seahawks.

Amazingly, coach Chuck Knox's bunch
pulled together, went 12–4, reached the play-
off semifinals, and sent seven players to the
Pro Bowl. Unfortunately, they start 1985 0–0
in the toughest division of the AFC.

That's the challenge facing Seattle — and
the Seahawks may well be up to it. Without Warner, the team was forced to throw the
ball a lot last year. With a healthy Warner
back in '85, they may well have their most
balanced attack ever.

The offensive line is most improved, with
tackles Ron Essink and Bob Cryder, guards
Edwin Bailey and Robert Pratt, and center

Blair Bush. Their backups are large fellows, too. It's a fine group, especially when Warner is available.

The running attack really needs Warner and Zach Dixon. Fullback David Hughes was the leading rusher with only 327 yards (Warner had 1,449 by himself a year earlier). No back started more than seven games, and the backups, such as Eric Lane (299 yards) and Dan Doornink (215 yards), were nothing to get excited about. Iowa's Owen Gill should help.

The passing game is in better shape. Steve Largent (74 catches) went to his fourth Pro Bowl, and Daryl Turner (35 catches) was an outstanding rookie. A healthy Paul Johns would help, but Knox isn't counting on him. Only Dan Marino had more TD passes than Seattle's Dave Krieg (32).

The Seahawks' takeaway-giveaway ratio of +24 and stingy defense led the way to the play-offs. The secondary features stars such as RCB Dave Brown and All-Pro SS Ken Easley, along with LCB Keith Simpson and FS John Harris.

The front-line defense — ends Jacob Green and much-improved Jeff Bryant, and noseman Joe Nash — is outstanding. LILB Shelton Robinson was the leading tackler (93), and LOLB Bruce Scholtz showed remarkable improvement against the run.

The offensive line could use a little help, but this club is ready to play with anyone — which is required of every team in the AFC West.

AFC West
LOS ANGELES RAIDERS
1984 Finish: Third
1985 Prediction: Second

Todd Christensen   **Rod Martin**

Just when the world thought the Raiders were set for their own version of *Dynasty*, Al Davis' gang flopped to third in the AFC West with a whammy thrown on them by the Seahawks.

Now the Silver and Black look to patch up the holes to climb back on the road to Super Bowl XX. Not that the cupboard is bare, for it certainly isn't. Their 11–5 record in '84 was good enough to win a division title in most NFL divisions — but not in the AFC West.

The Raiders have a real need at quarterback, where Jim Plunkett can no longer do it and Marc Wilson has yet to prove that he can. There's a need at wide receiver where speedy Cliff Branch is still the main man despite advancing "old" age, and the newcomers haven't met the test. The offensive line is beginning to thin its ranks, a surprise for Raider fans who always thought the group would never run out of talent.

There are also questions about the defensive line, particularly if end Greg Townsend and/or tackle Bill Pickel is dealt to fill other holes. End Lyle Alzado is nearing the wrap-up of his stellar career.

Still, the plusses are many. There aren't many tight ends in the class of Todd Christensen (80 catches, 1,007 yards). Marcus Allen (275 carries, 1,168 yards) is one of the most dazzling runners — inside and out, and he can also catch the football. Dokie Williams (22 catches, 509 yards) could be a future star at WR, even if Malcolm Barnwell (45 catches, 851 yards) doesn't meet Raider expectations. Speedy Jessie Hester could fit in.

The defense features the best CB combo in the league, with All-Pro Mike Haynes and all-timer Lester Hayes. Combined with safety Van McElroy, the backfield is super-tough. If Townsend and Pickel are around, Howie Long and friends should keep plenty of pressure on opposing QBs. Matt Millen, Rod Martin, and the rest of the linebacking crew are a talented bunch.

Sure there are some problems. But anyone who writes the Raiders off has probably been playing without a helmet. There's just too much strength on defense — and too many outstanding players — for coach Tom Flores' charges to be very far out of the chase in '85.

AFC West
DENVER BRONCOS
1984 Finish: First
1985 Prediction: Third

John Elway   Dave Studdard

Denver's offense is fair. Its defense takes advantage of opportunities. It has some players headed down hill. It probably has too many youngsters. And, thanks to hard work, a little good fortune, and some outstanding coaching, it is coming off its best season ever and going right back into the thick of the super-tough AFC West race.

Coach Dan Reeves never had fewer than 14 rookies on the Bronco squad a year ago on the way to a 13–3 mark. Credit QB John Elway (214 for 380, 2,598 yards, 18 TDs) for some of the improvement. Despite a lack of a good tight end and a slower-than-usual set of receivers, Elway began to show off the stuff that made him everyone's top choice out of Stanford.

The one-back offense is in decent shape

with Sammy Winder (296 carries, 1,153 yards) and explosive Gerald Willhite.

Speedy wide receivers are a major need to complement Steve Watson (69 catches, 1,170 yards). Butch Johnson, the ex-Cowboy, returns after his best season, with Clint Sampson expected back from the injury ranks. The offensive line, led by C Billy Bryan and T Dave Studdard, is excellent. RT Ken Lanier, RG Paul Howard, and LG Keith Bishop should all be back.

However, Denver really makes it on defense. The Broncos allowed only 241 points, second lowest in the league. Ends Rulon Jones and Barney Chavous combined for 18½ sacks, playing alongside noseman Rubin Carter.

A year's experience should help RILB Steve Busick, Denver's leading tackler, and LILB Rick Dennison, both of whom started as rookies. Tom Jackson, off another fine season, is beginning to show some signs of wear on the right outside, with Jim Ryan solid at left outside.

Corner Louis Wright (113 tackles) leads a tremendous secondary that includes Mike Harden at the opposite corner and future All-Pro Dennis Smith and Steve Foley at the safeties. The defensive backs had 24 of Denver's 31 intercepts and 10 of Denver's 24 fumble recoveries. Overall, the Broncs had eight defensive TDs in '84.

Despite a tough schedule and being in the AFC's toughest division, the Broncs should challenge again.

AFC West
KANSAS CITY CHIEFS
1984 Finish: Fourth
1985 Prediction: Fourth

Bill Kenney

Lloyd Burruss

The '84 Chiefs went 4–4 in the super-tough AFC West, which says that Kaycee has risen to the so-so level. With the Broncos, Seahawks, and Raiders to catch, they may be so-so again in '85.

Coach John Mackovic's team will be able to move the ball and score points through the air — perhaps as well as any team in the league. Their chances of putting together any kind of running attack is less likely.

Kaycee has decent depth at QB, with young Todd Blackledge backing up one of the NFL's best, Bill Kenney (53.5% completions, 15 TDs, 2,098 yards in 10 games after breaking a thumb).

The Chiefs are blessed with a great corps of receivers, led by Carlos Carson (57 catches, 1,078 yards) and Henry Marshall. They get plenty of support from Stephone Paige and Anthony Hancock, both of whom could start elsewhere. Tight ends Willie Scott and Walt Arnold are excellent.

The running game, on the other hand, is sickly. The loss of Theotis Brown (heart attack) makes a shaky situation worse. Herman Heard (684 yards) was a pleasant '84 surprise. Billy Jackson and Ken Lacy return at fullback, but much more is needed. North Carolina's Ethan Horton must be ready soon.

The front-line troops allowed only 33 sacks in '84, fourth lowest in the league. The middle of the line is outstanding, featuring guards Brad Budde and Tom Condon surrounding center Bob Rush. Matt Herkenhoff and David Lutz should return at tackle, with big help from John Alt.

The defense has some major strengths. End Art Still is one of the very best, and partner Mike Bell isn't too shabby. Noseman Bill Maas should return, although the Chiefs are looking for depth at that spot, with a possible return to a 4–3 set.

Kaycee is also set at safety, where Deron Cherry and Lloyd Burruss hang out. Both are excellent. Cornerbacks Albert Lewis and last year's rookie surprise, Kevin Ross, are adequate.

LB Jerry Blanton bounced back from back problems at midyear in '84, joining Gary Spani and John Zamberlin on the inside. Calvin Daniels will be joined by either Ken McAlister or Jeff Paine on the outside.

AFC West
SAN DIEGO CHARGERS
1984 Finish: Fifth
1985 Prediction: Fifth

Gill Byrd

Eric Sievers

The 1984 Chargers went 7–1 against non-AFC West teams. Unfortunately, they went 0–8 against division rivals. That 7–9 finish placed them in the West basement, a location that will be difficult to leave.

Key man on the '84 roster was the team doctor, who started treating fallen Chargers during the preseason minicamp and worked overtime through the campaign. (Example: San Diego lost three tight ends in four minutes of play.)

Speaking of TEs, a return by severely injured Kellen Winslow would help a Charger comeback. Otherwise, Eric Sievers and Pete Holohan will get the call. Wide man Charlie Joiner is the NFL's all-time receiver (657 catches), with Wes Chandler and Bobby Duckworth providing support.

They all get the ball from one of the NFL's best quarterbacks, Dan Fouts (3,740 yards, despite missing three games). Backup Ed Luther is off to the USFL, leaving Bruce Mathison and whomever else to sub for Fouts.

The running game is spelled Earnest Jackson (1,179 yards, the AFC's best) and not much more. Lionel James could help. The aging offensive line, which specializes in keeping opponents off the quarterback, returns former guard Ed White at tackle, Doug Wilkerson at guard, and Don Macek at center. Young guard Dennis McKnight even started two games at center in '84 when Macek was hurt. Sam Claphan had a good year at tackle. Ohio State's Jim Lachey should help.

The defense is in horrible shape. Up front, coach Don Coryell's troops play a 3-4, using Chuck Ehin and Keith Ferguson at the ends and Bill Elko in the middle, with help from Keith Guthrie. The linebacking is fair, featuring Woodrow Lowe and Linden King on the outside and Billy Ray Smith and Mike Green on the inside. There will be changes made, possibly including a healthy Mike Guendling.

In the backfield, look for more changes. Youngsters Danny Walters and Gill Byrd flopped in '84, leaving Lucious Smith and Bill Kay at the corners and Ken Greene and Tim Fox at safeties for '85. All of the above could stay or go on a moment's notice.

So could coach Coryell, if owner Alex Spanos loses his cool.

Richard Todd, who was expected to lead the Saints to the top of the NFL West, may not even start in '85.

National Football Conference Team Previews

NFC East
ST. LOUIS CARDINALS
1984 Finish: Third (tied)
1985 Prediction: First

Neil Lomax   E.J. Junior

At Busch Stadium, the star pitcher and catcher usually play for the baseball Cardinals. No more. The stick-out battery in St. Louis is pitcher Neil Lomax and catcher Roy "Jet Stream" Green, of the football Cardinals.

This dynamic duo nearly led the gridiron Birds into the play-offs, bowing out on the last play of the regular season. Meanwhile, 1985 Cardinal opponents have been quaking all spring and summer, fearful of their upcoming dates with the NFL's top pitch-catch combo. (Lomax threw for 4,619 yards a year ago, including 1,555 to Green.)

But the Cards are hardly a two-man show. The offensive line holds the key to future improvement. Tackle Tootie Robbins, guards Terry Stieve and Joe Bostic, and center Randy

Clark are moving toward the top class of NFL lines, though tackle Luis Sharpe signed with the USFL.

Green and fellow wide receiver Pat Tilley are a first-class pair, but they need help. Ottis Anderson (1,174 yards) and Stump Mitchell are satisfactory running backs, and both have become fine receivers. Overall, the offense must reduce its turnovers. The Big Red turned the ball over 16 times during a three-game November losing streak, which severely damaged their play-off hopes.

The Card defensive line, outstanding against the pass, fair against the run, must improve. RE Curtis Greer is the standout among a group that includes LE Al Baker and RT David Galloway. Greer had 14 sacks.

Star MLB E.J. Junior anchors a fine group. Some experts argue that Junior may be the best middle man in the game. He gets help from Thomas Howard and Charlie Baker.

In the secondary, free safety Benny Perrin is the key man. Only Junior made more tackles than Perrin in '84. Left corner Lionel Washington is a solid citizen. He was involved in more pass plays than any other Cardinal defensive back and was third among Card tacklers.

Coach Jim Hanifan hopes that the 1985 rookie crop is more productive than the 1984 group. He also looks for improvement by the special teams, which created problems a year ago. A play-off berth looks like a good bet.

NFC East
WASHINGTON REDSKINS
1984 Finish: First
1985 Prediction: Second

Dave Butz   Joe Theismann

The 1984 Redskins won the NFC East with numbers. No fewer than 63 players wore the famed burgundy and gold colors during the season, with 31 Redskins on injured reserve between the start of training camp and the final play-off game.

Credit Joe Gibbs with a super coaching job, while juggling the Skins' floating roster. With a little luck, the Skins may have an easier time defending in the NFC East. But don't count on it.

The offense must begin with the line, including tackles Mark May and All-Pro Joe Jacoby, guards Russ Grimm and possibly Ken Huff, and healthy center Jeff Bostic. The Jacoby-Grimm-Bostic trio may be the game's strongest.

QB Joe Theismann may have had better

years than '84, but he also owns enough courage for three or four NFL quarterbacks. No one knows RB John Riggins' condition from week to week. John is on the verge of retirement, but he'll probably keep going until he simply can't any longer. Last year he spent the week between games in traction in the hospital, getting ready for Sunday. Ex-Saint George Rogers is a great insurance policy.

Theismann's receivers are among the very best, including All-Pro Art Monk, ex-Raider Calvin Muhammad, Charlie Brown, oft-injured Clint Didier, and Don Warren. It's a first-rate group.

The Skins' defense occasionally bends, but rarely breaks. There's outstanding talent up front, with ends Charles Mann, Tony McGee, and Dexter Manley, and tackles Dave Butz, Darryl Grant, and Perry Brooks. Butz could well be the best of the lot, and that's not too shabby.

The Skin linebackers are like tigers. They gnaw, chew, grab, hold, and win. Again, there's decent depth with Mel Kaufman, Rich Milot, and Monte Coleman on the outside, and Neal Olkewicz and Larry Kubin on the inside.

Corners Darrell Green and Vernon Dean are one of the NFL's best duos, though the Skins could use some help at safety.

The kicking game is in reasonable shape, and the special teams are outstanding. It's tough to keep winning in the NFC East, but the Skins are equipped to do it.

61

NFC East
NEW YORK GIANTS
1984 Finish: Second
1985 Prediction: Third

Phil Simms   **Mark Haynes**

"The Giants," says 49er coach Bill Walsh, "are a team of the future."

"The future," according to veteran coach George Allen, "is now."

That's the problem facing the Giants following their second play-off season in two decades. Coach Bill Parcells' team made giant strides (what else?) in going from a 3–12–1 mark to a berth in the NFC semifinals. The question now is: Are the Giants for real?

We think so. The club has genuine stars in OLB Lawrence Taylor, ILB Harry Carson, and CB Mark Haynes. The Giants have solid pros in QB Phil Simms (53.7% completions, 22 TDs, 4,044 yards) and nose tackle Jim Burt. And there's a wealth of young talent that has an additional year of experience.

The running game is still only so-so. Leading rusher Rob Carpenter (250 carries for 795 yards) got late-season help from speedy Joe Morris (133 for 510 yards), but not enough to make the Giants a real overland threat. Ex-Jersey General (USFL) Maurice Carthon and top draft choice George Adams should make real contributions.

The young offensive line may miss C Kevin Belcher, slow in recovering from an off-season auto crash. But there is potential there, with Ts William Roberts and Karl Nelson and Gs Bill Ard (sorely missed in the play-offs) and Chris Godfrey.

Improved receivers, again mostly rookies and second-year men, helped Simms to his best season a year ago. That group includes Bob Johnson, Lionel Manuel, and tight end Zeke Mowatt, along with vets Earnest Gray and all-purpose back Tony Galbreath.

Defense is still the name of the Giants' game. Rookie LBs Carl Banks and Gary Reasons joined the Taylor-Carson duo last year, backing up fellows such as DE Leonard Marshall, Curtis McGriff, and Jim Burt.

The Giants need some defensive backfield depth. CB Kenny Daniel couldn't do it when Haynes went down late last season. There's potential in the secondary, though, with young Perry Williams another future All-Pro at the corner. S Terry Kinard is solid, too.

K Ali Haji-Sheikh and P Dave Jennings must improve for the Giants to move up.

NFC East
DALLAS COWBOYS
1984 Finish: Third (tied)
1985 Prediction: Fourth

Everson Walls   Tony Hill

Coach Tom Landry can't wait for the '85 season to begin. After all, it has to be better than 1984, when the 'Pokes missed the play-offs for only the second time in 19 years.

Actually, things could have been worse. We predicted that the Cowboys would miss the play-offs, yet they came closer than they had a right to. They were hit hard by injuries (on and off the field), retirements, USFL departures, trades, and other problems too numerous to mention. But a victory in either of the last two games could have produced that play-off berth, and Dallas was in both games to the end.

By opening day '85, Landry will probably have solved his QB problem. The battle between Danny White and Gary Hogeboom bothered the club all last season, with

White playing less but rating higher.

Solving the QB situation is hardly Landry's only headache. A healthy offensive line would help, too. Every starter missed some time in '85, led by tackle Jim Cooper, who tore his ankle and knee on the dance floor. There are some solid citizens among the group, including tackle Phil Pozderac, guard Kurt Petersen, and center Tom Rafferty. Herb Scott retired.

Speedy Tony Hill and Doug Donley should provide excellent targets for the quarterback, whoever he is. Tony Dorsett (1,189 yards) remains a constant threat at the deep back spot.

The defense will miss Billy Cannon, Jr., whose rookie-year neck injury has ended his career. But Randy "Manster" White is coming off possibly his best season, and young Jim Jeffcoat showed great promise, finishing second in sacks behind White. LT John Dutton and LE Too Tall Jones are aging.

Michael Downs, the free safety, is an All-Pro and the 'Pokes' top tackler. There's nothing wrong with Everson Walls, the star left corner.

Landry has some outstanding young talent such as MLB Steve DeOssie, CB Victor Scott, and TE Brian Salonen. But the Cowboys always have fine young talent.

Dallas' biggest problem may be the fine NFC East, possibly the NFC's toughest division. The Cowboys play seven 1984 playoff teams, including champion San Francisco at Candlestick.

NFC East
PHILADELPHIA EAGLES
1984 Finish: Fifth
1985 Prediction: Fifth

Jerry Robinson

Mike Quick

The '84 Eagles weren't sure who the owner was, weren't sure where they'd be playing in '85, and weren't lucky enough to be playing in an easier division.

Coming off a 5–11 season, the Eagles were a much better football team, yet finished at only 6–9–1. It could easily have gone the opposite way, but bad teams generally aren't lucky.

Things should be a lot more stable in '85, and the schedule is much easier. But the record might not improve. There are no enormous holes to fill, though an offensive lineman or two would help, and so would an inside linebacker. The ILB would allow coach Marion Campbell to shift star Jerry Robinson to the outside.

It wouldn't hurt to improve the running

game, too. Leading rusher Wilbert Montgomery averaged only 3.9 yards per carry (789 yards overall). Worse, the backs scored only three TDs on the ground.

If Ron Jaworski is still around, it won't be for long. Jaws has been hit plenty in his Eagle days, including 60 sacks (shared with Joe Pisarcik) last season.

That speaks volumes on the state of the offensive line. The last great Eagle tackle, Jerry Sisemore, is talking retirement. But even if he plays, he's 34 years old. Top draftee Kevin Allen should start.

The receiving corps, on the other hand, is a major asset. Kenny Jackson was going great until a separated shoulder finished his season at midyear. That put extra pressure on speedy Mike Quick (61 catches, 1,049 yards). TE John Spagnola was the top receiver, and blocking TE Vyto Kab had nine catches, three for TDs.

The defense is in much better shape. The front line set a club record with 60 sacks, thanks to ends Greg Brown and Dennis Harrison and nose tackle Kenny Clarke.

The secondary hits about as hard as any group in the NFL. Safeties Wes Hopkins and Ray Ellis have loosened a fair share of opponents' teeth.

The kicking game is in good hands (and feet) with young punter Mike Horan and second-year placekicker Paul McFadden (30 FGs, leading the league).

With the easier schedule, the record could improve, but the play-offs are still a dream.

NFC Central
CHICAGO BEARS
1984 Finish: First
1985 Prediction: First

Richard Dent   **Dan Hampton**

Despite a 10–6 season and an NFC Central title, coach Mike Ditka was under a ton of pressure as 1984 ended. Now Chicago fans' hopes are set even higher, with a Super Bowl in their dreams.

The talent is there, especially if QB Jim McMahon stays healthy. The ex-Brigham Young star had two sets of records last year: passing and medical. On the passing side, it was 85 for 143, 1,146 yards, and 8 TDs. On the medical side, it was a broken throwing hand, a bruised back, and a lacerated kidney. His backup, Steve Fuller, did well, except for two shoulder separations.

The running game is in the capable hands (and feet) of Walter "Sweetness" Payton, the NFL's all-time leading rusher and good guy. He even got a shot at backup quarterback late in the season and did reasonably well, running most of the time. Does he have another 1,684-yard rushing season in him? Let's see.

The offensive line is in wonderful shape from left to right with Jim Covert, Mark Bortz, Jay Hilgenberg, Kurt Becker, and Keith Van Horne.

At least four of the defensive starters were All-Pros or close to it. The right side of the line is particularly strong, with end Richard Dent and tackle Dan Hampton. And there's nothing wrong with the combo of Mike Hartenstine and Steve McMichael on the left. And what about top draftee 318-pound William "Refrigerator" Perry?

In making a major improvement against the pass, middle linebacker Mike Singletary has gone to the head of the class of NFL MLBs. Otis Wilson is a tower of strength on the left, with Al Harris equally prepared on the right.

Strong safety Todd Bell heads a backfield foursome that includes Mike Richardson and Leslie Frazier at the corners and hard-hitting Gary Fencik at free safety.

If the Bears have a weakness, it's in the pass-receiving department. Wide man Dennis McKinnon is most reliable, while sprinter Willie Gault, always a deep threat, seems to have trouble hanging on to balls thrown over the middle.

With a little consistency and a little luck, it could be a wonderful fall in the Windy City.

NFC Central
TAMPA BAY BUCCANEERS
1984 Finish: Third
1985 Prediction: Second

Dave Logan   Scot Brantley

The Bucs have a Culverhouse (the team
owners), a powerhouse (the overall offense), and a Kevin House (the top receiver
with 76 catches and 1,005 yards). What they
don't have is a defense, which keeps them
from challenging for the NFC Central title.

For years coach John McKay's club fea-
tured a smothering defense and little offense. In McKay's last year, the offense
finally put it together, with the potent rushing (1,544 yards) and receiving (85 catches)
of James Wilder. Wilder even made a better
quarterback out of Steve DeBerg (60.5%
completions, 19 TDs), who won the job from
Jack Thompson early last season.

New coach Leeman Bennett inherits the
solid Buc offense, which should improve as
the offensive line improves. Ron Heller, the

starter at right tackle as a rookie last year, was a pleasant surprise. The rest of the group is coming fast, with Sean Farrell and Steve Courson at the guards, Ken Kaplan or Gene Sanders at left tackle, and Steve Wilson at center. Guard Glenn Bujnoch and center Randy Grimes should see plenty of action.

Even the kicking game is in its best shape ever, with Obed Ariri setting Buc marks in field goals (19) and scoring (95 points), and Frank Garcia as the punter.

Actually, the defense is in decent shape. Good health is the key. An auto accident, which injured star right outside backer Hugh Green, really set back the Buc defense in '84. When he's in there with All-Pro RE Lee Roy Selmon, the Bucs are superstrong on that side. A healthy linebacking corps could help the Bucs move up. Left outside LB Cecil Johnson missed much of '84 with a knee injury, and inside men Jeff Davis and Scot Brantley suffered with shoulder woes all season. The youngsters, such as linebackers Chris Washington and Keith Browner, learned well.

The secondary needs shoring up, though better play up front should relieve some of the pressure. Left safety Mark Cotney had five interceptions last year, and only Jeremiah Castille (with three) had more than one.

Only the AFC Central was as weak as the NFC Central a year ago, which provides some hope for rookie coach Bennett.

NFC Central
DETROIT LIONS
1984 Finish: Fourth
1985 Prediction: Third

Keith Dorney

William Gay

Darryl Rogers couldn't have picked a better time to become head coach of the Lions. The former Arizona State boss arrives on the heels of a horrid 4–11–1 season that, if anything, was worse than the record shows. Still, there seems to be enough talent on board that Rogers has a shot at turning the record around in '85.

The big if, of course, is the state of Billy Sims' health. The Lions' rushing star went down with a knee injury at midseason, with 687 yards and a 5.4 yards-per-carry average under his belt. FB James Jones, the club's offensive MVP, took up some of the slack, finishing with 77 pass receptions and 532 rushing yards. Meanwhile QB Gary Danielson, who wasn't expected to see much action, fell into the starting job and finished with one of his best all-round efforts. He completed a club-record 252 passes for 3,076 yards.

A healthy offensive line should help Rogers and his team. Tackle Rich Strenger and center Steve Mott went out early last year, and the line never recovered. Florida's Lomas Brown should fit right in. Among the receivers, quick Leonard Thompson (50 catches, 773 yards) should join with Mark Nichols (a late-season starter) to provide excellent targets.

Defensively there's plenty of work to do. Hopefully, Bill Gay will do a better job at end, if Rogers doesn't switch him back to tackle, where he was an All-Pro. Overall, the pass rush needs much improvement; there wasn't much last year until late in the season.

Middle linebacker Ken Fantetti was the Lions' outstanding defender a year ago, despite missing training camp. On the outside, Garry Cobb and Jimmy Williams, who started every game in '84, provide decent help.

Lion-watchers point to breakdowns in the defensive secondary as a key cause of 1984 difficulties. Neither corner Bruce McNorton nor safety William Graham were particularly outstanding. Bobby Watkins and Alvin Hall are adequate.

A fairly tough schedule, with most of the tougher opponents at home, is another challenge for Rogers, who must convince his players that they can win in the NFC Central.

NFC Central
GREEN BAY PACKERS
1984 Finish: Second
1985 Prediction: Fourth

James Lofton

George Cumby

Statistics can fool you. The Packers finished at 8–8 for the second straight year in '84. But Forrest Gregg's club was much improved from the '83 edition.

In fact, Green Bay's 7–1 record over the last half of last season provides great hope for '85. Coach Gregg has turned the Pack into a power team, with excellent results.

The key is the continued solid play of the defense. Ends Alphonso Carreker and Donnie Humphrey start their second year, after proving especially strong against the run. They get plenty of help from noseman Terry Jones and inside backer Randy Scott, a major surprise.

The secondary is much improved, with corners Tim Lewis and Mark Lee proving to be solid pros, and safeties Tom Flynn and

Mark Murphy showing great strength. Flynn, with nine interceptions, led the NFC as a rookie.

Still, for the Pack to make the play-offs, they'll need a stronger inside pass rush and more big plays from the defense.

Offensively, the Packers will rely on the rebuilt line that carried them through the last eight games. This means the return of Ron Hallstrom and Tim Huffman at the guards, where they stood out after winning starting spots four games into the season. Tackles Greg Koch and Karl Swanke are both solid, with Swanke coming off his best year. Center Larry McCarren does a professional job.

There are potential problems at quarterback. Aging Lynn Dickey, who played hurt most of last year, can do the job, as long as he's healthy. He was the league's seventh-ranked passer in '84. The Packers hope that young Randy Wright, who suffered torn knee ligaments last December, will be ready to step in when needed. If not, the Pack may have to shop around.

RB Eddie Lee Ivery (99 carries, 552 yards) was a 1984 success story, after '83 drug problems. Solid fullback Gerry Ellis returns as the leading rusher (581 yards) behind the improved offensive line.

The kicking game must be improved, but the Packers have come a long way, baby, and a real shot at the play-offs — and a possible conference title — is waiting for them in '85.

NFC Central
MINNESOTA VIKINGS
1984 Finish: Fifth
1985 Prediction: Fifth

Darrin Nelson   **Greg Coleman**

The Vikings believe that Bud Grant can do what all the king's horses and all the king's men couldn't. The long-time Vike coach is being asked to reassemble a shattered team that sank to new depths under one-year coach Les Steckel a year ago.

Grant, who's intense on the outside and supercool on the inside, returns to the helm after a brief absence of 16 games, only three of which were Viking victories.

Problem is, the Vikings weren't all that spectacular during Grant's last six seasons (less than .500) and his year away saw the defense turn dreadful. It allowed 484 points per game last year, including a 241–79 gap in the final six contests.

A look at last year's roster is meaningless. The defensive line, including fellows like nose tackle Charlie Johnson and end Doug Martin, have done reasonably well in the past. But they couldn't cut it during the Steckel era. Worse, Minny's top draft pick of '84 was a defensive end, Keith Millard. But he signed with the USFL when the Vikes failed to post the bucks. Tight spending is another major Viking problem.

Meanwhile, the linebackers, including vets Sammy Blair and Scott Studwell, are aging. And the secondary has enough holes to make Swiss cheese jealous.

The offense is in somewhat better shape. Quarterback Tommy Kramer can do the job — when he's healthy. But he missed much of '83 with a knee injury and '84 with a shoulder separation. If the Vikings can pick up a great young passer, Kramer could be dealt.

Alfred Anderson, who came fast as a rookie (he led Viking rushers with 773 yards) could pair with Darrin Nelson or Ted Brown (who was suspended by Grant in '83).

One advantage for Grant in '85 is Grant. Some of the Vikings who retired or were cut by Steckel could be back. For example, Terry LeCount could return at wide receiver, where Minny desperately needs help.

If love and respect for the head coach motivates players to perform over their heads, the Vikings could really soar this season. Grant has won love and honor, especially after the players got a single dose of Steckel. But this job seems too much for Bud.

NFC West
SAN FRANCISCO 49ERS
1984 Finish: First
1985 Prediction: First

Joe Montana   Ronnie Lott

It was a pleasant off-season for 49er coach Bill Walsh — or "The Genius" as some call him. Walsh may not be a genius, but he has the kind of talent that makes him look awfully brilliant most of the time.

Off an 18–1 season and a Super Bowl rout of Miami, Walsh did what everyone expected him to do this off-season — very little. Oh sure, the Niners might look to strengthen themselves with more depth at fullback, cornerback, tackle, defensive end, or wide receiver. Inside linebacker Jack Reynolds was talking retirement, which might hurt a bit. But there isn't a coach in the league who wouldn't gladly swap problems with Walsh.

Start with the potent offense and its leader, Joe Montana. The QB hit on 64.6% of his passes last year, for 3,630 yards and 28 TDs. His leading rusher, RB Wendell Tyler (1,262 yards), and leading receiver, FB Roger Craig (71 catches), will rejoin him in the Niner backfield.

Walsh may have to go shopping for a backup wide receiver if the fastest hurdler ever, Renaldo Nehemiah, doesn't make it soon. Dwight Clark (52 catches) and Freddie Solomon (40) need help, possibly from top draft choice Jerry Rice.

Up front, only All-Pro T Keith Fahnhorst is getting on in years. The rest of the crowd, T Bubba Paris, Gs John Ayers and Randy Cross, and C Fred Quillan, should be protecting Montana for a long while.

Defensively, there are a couple of questions. Reynolds' status is one. Nickel back Tim Collier (off a torn Achilles tendon) is another. The secondary is loaded, with Pro Bowlers Ronnie Lott and Eric Wright at the corners and Carlton Williamson and Dwight Hicks at safeties.

Up front, age could creep up on Fred Dean, but the pass-rush is in fine shape with ends Lawrence Pillers and Dwaine Board and nose tackle Manu Tuiasosopo. Without Reynolds, either Jim Fahnhorst (brother of Keith) or Mike Walter could join outside backers Dan Bunz and Keena Turner and inside man Riki Ellison.

Walsh will be on the lookout for a (third-and-one) back and a couple of other situation players, but basically the 49ers are set. Their target: New Orleans next January.

NFC West
LOS ANGELES RAMS
1984 Finish: Second
1985 Prediction: Second

Drew Hill   Bill Bain

The 1984 Rams proved that even Superman, RB Eric Dickerson, isn't enough to guarantee an NFL championship. The goggled Dickerson dazzled every opponent on the way to 2,105 record-breaking yards and did everything coach John Robinson expected during a 10–6 season.

Still, by failing against the Giants in the wild-card play-off game, the Rams proved that they still have some growing up to do, particularly with their passing game. As a result, ex-Canadian star Dieter Brock joins this year's QB Derby, with Vince Ferragamo and Jeff Kemp.

Whoever wins that one will have some outstanding receivers to throw to. You can't do much better than wide receivers Henry Ellard, Drew Hill, and Ron Brown, who averaged 21 yards per catch in '84. Trouble was, they caught only 71 balls between them. Blame that in some measure on the coaching staff's lack of faith in Kemp, who was rarely allowed to throw deep.

The offensive line, which gets major credit for Dickerson's star performance, has plenty of life left, especially if Jackie Slater returns healthy. Bill Bain is one of the best at right tackle, with Slater and Irv Pankey battling on the left. The rest of the group includes guards Dennis Harrah and Kent Hill, along with center Doug Smith.

The defense, which was hurt deeply by injuries in '84, must improve for the Rams to challenge the champion 49ers in the NFC West. Last season's hospital list included safeties Johnnie Johnson, Nolan Cromwell, and Eric Harris; linebacker George Andrews; and end Jack Youngblood (who may be through). Still, the Rams managed to keep things together most of the time. Credit folks such as end Reggie Doss, noseman Greg Meisner, inside backers Carl Ekern and Jim Collins, outside men Mel Owens and Mike Wilcher, and corners Gary Green and LeRoy Irvin for a job well done. Backup noseman Charley DeJurnett and end Gary Jeter provide excellent depth.

With the kicking game in reasonable shape, a renewed defense, and a real passing game, there's no reason why the Rams can't make another play-off visit. Catching the Niners, who were five games better in '84, is another story.

NFC West
ATLANTA FALCONS
1984 Finish: Fourth
1985 Prediction: Third

Gerald Riggs　　　　　　　　　**Mike Kenn**

The Falcons are all set for '85 — at running back and along the defensive line. Other than that, who knows?

Atlanta comes off a horrid 4–12 season with tons of question marks, an injured quarterback, a 39-year-old center, and an offensive line that allowed Falcon throwers to be sacked 67 times.

Let's start with the few plusses. Despite the loss of RB William Andrews for the season, the running game was left in good shape with Gerald Riggs (1,486 yards) and Lynn Cain.

Wide receiver is another strong spot, with Stacey Bailey (67 catches, tops on the club), veteran Alfred Jenkins, and Floyd Hodge. And Cliff Benson stepped right in at the halfback spot and took over.

The defensive line features young Rick Bryan, Gary Burley, Andrew Provence, Don Smith, and Mike Pitts. It's a decent group.

But none of the above could prevent a nine-game losing streak, which turned a .500 team into a big loser. Backup quarterback Mike Moroski, who filled in for the injured Steve Bartkowski, proved that he couldn't do the job, though he might have to again in '85.

The defensive secondary didn't do the Falcons much good last year. Only safety Tom Pridemore didn't commit at least one interference penalty. Corners Bobby Butler and James Britt and safety Kenny Johnson will try to reduce their loose play in '85.

Atlanta hopes that John Rade can rejoin the linebacking corps of David Frye, Buddy Curry, and Al Richardson.

The quarterback situation will improve if the offensive line improves. The front five was called for holding 23 times a year ago, with only guards R.C. Thielemann and John Scully escaping notice. (Actually, Scully was tabbed once.) Tackles Mike Kenn and Brett Miller will face new pressures in '85, while Atlanta looks for aging center Jeff Van Note's replacement. Pitt's Bill Fralic will help immediately.

If Bartkowski, Andrews, and wide receiver Billy Johnson return from their disabling injuries, the Falcons will take a major step in returning to the NFC West race. But with the Rams and Forty-Niners light-years ahead, that return could take a while.

NFC West
NEW ORLEANS SAINTS
1984 Finish: Third
1985 Prediction: Fourth

Dave Waymer

Richard Todd

Eighteen seasons of losing finally caught up with original Saints' owner John Mecom. The high hopes of 1984 slipped into another 7–9 disappointment, and Mecom immediately decided to unload the club.

That puts additional pressure on coach Bum Phillips, who probably has to win in '85 — or else!

Frankly, Bum could be in trouble. The man with the cowboy hat and boots points to severe injury problems, especially along the offensive line, as the key to New Orleans' woes in '84. He has a point, though the Saints have other problems, too. Consider, however, that Steve Korte started the opener at center, then played 13 games at guard, and Kelvin Clark played every position except center. Okay, Bum.

The quarterback derby wasn't much to write home about. Richard Todd should still be No. 1, though Dave Wilson looked fairly good in the final games of the season. The Saints consider that position safe.

The Earl Campbell trade paid no dividends. George Rogers (now with the Redskins) continued to be the rushing leader (914 yards on 239 tough carries), with offensive MVP Hokie Gajan ready to do anything. He was the team's leading receiver (35 passes), nonkicking scorer (42 points), per-carry-average runner (6.0 yards per try).

New Orleans may well have better talent on defense. Linebacker Rickey Jackson should be an NFC Pro Bowler every year. Defensive end Bruce Clark is in that class, too. Jackson was the NFC's No. 1 sacking linebacker a year ago with 12. Clark chipped in with 10½ sacks.

The linebacking is first-rate. Whitney Paul joins Jackson on the outside, with Dirt Winston and Dr. Jim Kovach on the inside. The secondary is professional, especially corners Dave Waymer and Johnnie Poe. Safeties Russell Gary and Frank Wattelet get the job done.

The kicking game is in able hands. Place-kicker Morten Andersen didn't get to prove how good he is. But experts rate him highly. Rookie punter Brian Hansen (43.8 yards) punted himself into the Pro Bowl.

As the song says, it's now or never for Bum. With the strength of the NFC West, never is more like it.

NFL
Draft List

The following abbreviations are used to identify the players' positions:

OFFENSE — T = tackle; G = guard; C = center; QB = quarterback; RB = running back; WR = wide receiver; TE = tight end.

DEFENSE — DE = defensive end, DT = defensive tackle; LB = linebacker; DB = defensive back.

SPECIAL TEAMS — P = punter; K = placekicker; KR = kick returner.

The number preceding the player's name indicates the overall position in which he was drafted.

Atlanta Falcons
2, Bill Fralic, T, Pittsburgh. 45, Mike Gann, DE, Notre Dame. 89, Emile Harry, WR, Stanford. 152, Reggie Pleasant, DB, Clemson. 201, Ashley Lee, DB, Virginia. 215, Ronnie Washington, LB, Northeast Louisiana. 228, Micah Moon, LB, North Carolina. 257, Brent Martin, C, Stanford. 284, John Ayres, DB, Illinois. 313, Ken Whisenhunt, TE, Georgia Tech.

Buffalo Bills

1, Bruce Smith, DE, Virginia Tech. 14, Derrick Burroughs, DB, Memphis State. 29, Mark Traynowicz, T, Nebraska. 42, Chris Burkett, WR, Jackson State. 57, Frank Reich, QB, Maryland. 63, Hal Garner, LB, Utah State. 85, Andre Reed, WR, Kutztown (Pa.) State. 112, Dale Hellestrae, T, Southern Methodist. 130, Jimmy Teal, WR, Texas A&M. 141, Mike Hamby, DT, Utah State. 169, Ron Pitts, DB, UCLA. 197, Jacque Robinson, RB, Washington. 225, Glenn Jones, DB, Norfolk State. 253, Chris Babyar, G, Illinois. 282, James Seawright, LB, South Carolina. 333, Paul Woodside, K, West Virginia.

Chicago Bears

22, William Perry, DT, Clemson. 49, Reggie Phillips, DB, SMU. 78, James Maness, WR, TCU. 105, Kevin Butler, K, Georgia. 190, Charles Bennett, DE, Southwest Louisiana. 217, Steve Buxton, T, Indiana State. 249, Thomas Sanders, RB, Texas A&M. 273, Pat Coryatt, DT, Baylor. 302, James Morrissey, LB, Michigan State.

Cincinnati Bengals

13, Eddie Brown, WR, Miami. 25, Emannuel King, LB, Alabama. 43, Carl Zander, LB, Tennessee. 70, Sean Thomas, DB, TCU. 97, Anthony Tuggle, DB, Nicholis State. 127, Tony Degrate, DT, Texas. 129, Lee Davis, DB, Mississippi. 148, Eric Stokes, T, Northeastern. 154, Keith Lester, TE, Murray State. 172, Kim Locklin, RB, New Mexico State. 181, Joe Walter, T, Texas Tech. 211, Dave Strobel, LB, Iowa. 238, Keith Cruise, DE, Northwestern. 265, Bernard King, LB, Syracuse. 296, Harold Stanfield, TE, Mississippi College. 322, Louis Garza, T, New Mexico State.

Cleveland Browns

35, Greg Allen, RB, Florida State. 147, Mark Krerowicz, G, Ohio State. 175, Reginald Langhorne, WR, Elizabeth City State. 203, Fred Banks, WR, Liberty Baptist. 259, Larry Williams, G, Notre Dame. 287,

Travis Tucker, TE, Southern Connecticut. 315, Shane Swanson, WR, Nebraska.

Dallas Cowboys

17, Kevin Brooks, DE, Michigan. 44, Jesse Penn, LB, Virginia Tech. 76, Crawford Kerr, G, Florida. 103, Robert Lavette, RB, Georgia Tech. 114, Herschel Walker, RB, Georgia. 119, Matt Darwin, G, Texas A&M. 144, Kurt Ploeger, DE, Gustavus Adolphus. 157, Matt Moran, G, Stanford. 178, Karl Powe, WR, Alabama State. 184, Jim Herrmann, DE, Brigham Young. 216, Leon Gonzalez, WR, Bethune-Cookman. 243, Scott Strasburger, LB, Nebraska. 270, Joe Jones, TE, Virginia Tech. 297, Neal Dellocono, LB, UCLA. 324, Karl Jordan, LB, Vanderbilt.

Denver Broncos

26, Steve Sewell, RB, Oklahoma. 31, Vance Johnson, WR, Arizona. 54, Simon Fletcher, DE, Houston. 110, Keli McGregor, TE, Colorado State. 139, Billy Hinson, G, Florida. 194, Dallas Cameron, DT, Miami. 222, Eric Riley, DB, Florida State. 250, Daryl Smith, DB, North Alabama. 269, Buddy Funck, QB, New Mexico. 278, Ron Anderson, LB, SMU. 306, Gary Rolle, WR, Florida. 334, Dan Lynch, G, Washington State.

Detroit Lions

6, Lomas Brown, T, Florida. 34, Kevin Glover, C, Maryland. 62, James Johnson, LB, San Diego State. 90, Kevin Hancock, LB, Baylor. 118, Joe McIntosh, RB, North Carolina State. 146, Stan Short, G, Penn State. 174, Anthony Staten, DB, Angelo State. 202, Scotty Caldwell, RB, Texas-Arlington. 230, June James, LB, Texas. 258, Clayton Beauford, WR, Auburn. 286, Kevin Harris, DB, Georgia. 314, Mike Weaver, G, Georgia.

Green Bay Packers

7, Ken Ruettgers, T, USC. 71, Rich Moran, G, San Diego State. 98, Walter Stanley, WR, Mesa (Ariz.) 125, Brian Noble, LB, Arizona State. 155, Mark Lewis, TE, Texas A&M. 171 Eric Wilson, LB, Maryland. 182, Gary Ellerson, RB, Wisconsin. 209, Ken Stills, DB, Wisconsin. 239, Morris Johnson, G, Alabama A&M. 266, Ronnie Burgess, DB, Wake Forest. 294, Joe Shield, QB, Trinity (Conn.). 323, Jim Meyer, P, Arizona State.

Houston Oilers

3, Ray Childress, DE, Texas A&M. 11, Richard Johnson, DB, Wisconsin. 36, Richard Byrd, DE, Southern Mississippi. 82, Mike Kelley, C, Notre Dame. 87, Tom Briehl, LB, Stanford. 133, Frank Bush, LB, North Carolina State. 138, Lee Johnson, K, Brigham Young. 153, Joe Krakoski, LB, Washington. 170, Mike Akiu, WR, Hawaii. 199, Chuck Thomas, C, Oklahoma. 226, Steve Tasker, KR, Northwestern. 255, Mike Golic, DE, Notre Dame. 281, Willie Drewrey, WR, West Virginia. 311, Mark Vonder Haar, DT, Minnesota.

Indianapolis Colts

5, Duane Bickett, LB, USC. 32, Don Anderson, DB, Purdue. 61, Anthony Young, DB, Temple. 88, Willie Broughton, DE, Miami. 117, Roger Caron, T, Harvard. 173, James Harbour, WR, Mississippi. 200, Ricky Nichols, WR, East Carolina. 229, Mark Boyer, TE, USC. 256, Andre Pinesett, DT, Cal State-Fullerton. 312, David Burnette, T, Arkansas Central.

Kansas City Chiefs

15, Ethan Horton, RB, North Carolina. 41, Jon Hayes, TE, Iowa. 99, Bob Olderman, G, Virginia. 126, Bruce King, RB, Purdue. 149, Jonathon Bostic, DB, Bethune-Cookman. 180, Vince Thomson, DE, Missouri Western. 183, David Heffernan, G, Miami. 210, Ira Hillary, WR, South Carolina. 237, Mike Armentrout, DB, Southwest Missouri. 267, Jeff Smith, RB, Nebraska. 293, Chris Jackson, C, SMU. 321, Harper Le Bel, C, Colorado State.

Los Angeles Raiders

23, Jessie Hester, WR, Florida State. 79, Tim Moffett, WR, Mississippi. 80, Stefon Adams, DB, East Carolina. 107, Jamie Kimmel, LB, Syracuse. 135, Dan Reeder, RB, Delaware. 143, Rusty Hillger, QB, Oklahoma State.

186, Kevin Belcher, T, Wisconsin. 188, Mark Pattison, WR, Washington. 191, Bret Clark, DB, Nebraska. 192, Nick Haden, C, Penn State. 220, Leonard Wingate, DT, South Carolina State. 246, Chris Sydnor, DB, Penn State. 275, Reggie McKenzie, LB, Tennessee. 276, Albert Myres, DB, Tulsa. 303, Steve Strachan, RB, Boston College. 332, Raymond Polk, DB, Oklahoma State.

Los Angeles Rams

21, Jerry Gray, DB, Texas. 50, Chuck Scott, WR, Vanderbilt. 77, Dale Hatcher, P, Clemson. 113, Kevin Greene, LB, Auburn. 161, Mike Young, WR, UCLA. 162, Damone Johnson, TE, Cal-Poly Obispo. 189, Danny Bradley, RB, Oklahoma. 218, Marion McIntyre, RB, Pittsburgh. 245, Gary Swanson, LB, Cal Poly-Obispo. 274, Duval Love, G, UCLA. 285, Doug Flutie, QB, Boston College. 301, Kevin Brown, DB, Northwestern.

Miami Dolphins

27, Lorenzo Hampton, RB, Florida. 65, George Little, DT, Iowa. 83, Alex Moyer, LB, Northwestern. 91, Mike Smith, DB, UTEP. 111, Jeff Dellenbach, T, Wisconsin. 145, George Shorthose, WR, Missouri. 167, Ron Davenport, RB, Louisville. 195, Fuad Reveiz, K, Tennessee. 223, Dan Sharp, TE, TCU. 251, Adam Hinds, DB, Oklahoma State. 279, Mike Pendleton, DB, Indiana. 307, Mike Jones, RB, Tulane. 335, Ray Noble, DB, California.

Minnesota Vikings

4, Chris Doleman, LB, Pittsburgh. 30, Issiac Holt, DB, Alcorn State. 59, Kirk Lowdermilk, C, Ohio State. 60, Tim Meamber, LB, Washington. 66, Tim Long, T, Memphis State. 86, Buster Rhymes, WR, Oklahoma. 106, Kyle Morrell, DB, Brigham Young. 115, Mark MacDonald, C, Boston College. 142, Steve Bono, QB, UCLA. 164, Tim Newton, DT, Florida. 198, Nikita Blair, LB, Texas-El Paso. 227, Jamie Covington, RB, Syracuse. 254, Juan Johnson, WR, Langston (Okla.). 283, Tim Williams, DB, North Carolina A&T. 310, Byron Jones, DT, Tulsa.

New England Patriots

28, Trevor Matich, C, Brigham Young. 48, Garin Veris, DE, Stanford. 52, Jim Bowman, DB, Central Michigan. 56, Ben Thomas, DE, Auburn. 84, Audrey McMillian, DB, Houston. 102, Tom Toth, T, Western Michigan. 108, Gerard Phelan, WR, Boston College. 224, Milford Hodge, DT, Washington State. 295, Paul Lewis, RB, Boston University. 328, Tony Mumford, RB, Penn State.

New Orleans Saints

24, Alvin Toles, LB, Tennessee. 38, Darren Gilbert, T, Fullerton State. 68, Jack Del Rio, LB, USC. 95, Billy Allen, DB, Florida State. 179, Eric Martin, WR, LSU. 206, Joe Kohlbrand, DE, Miami. 236, Earl Johnson, DB, South Carolina. 320, Treg Songy, DB, Tulane.

New York Giants

19, George Adams, RB, Kentucky. 46, Stacy Robinson, WR, North Dakota State. 58, Tyrone Davis, DB, Clemson. 73, Brian Johnston, C, North Carolina. 100, Mark Bavaro, TE, Notre Dame. 132, Tracy Henderson, WR, Iowa State. 159, Jack Oliver, G, Memphis State. 165, Mark Pembrook, DB, Cal-State Fullerton. 213, Lee Rouson, RB, Colorado. 240, Frank Wright, DT, South Carolina. 272, Gregg Dubroc, LB, LSU. 299, Allen Young, DB, Virginia Tech. 326, Herb Welch, DB, UCLA.

New York Jets

10, Al Toon, WR, Wisconsin. 40, Lester Lyles, DB, Virginia. 67, Donnie Elder, DB, Memphis State. 94, Doug Allen, WR, Arizona State. 120, Troy Benson, LB, Pittsburgh. 124, Brian Luft, DT, USC. 134, Tony Smith, WR, San Jose State. 151, Jeff Deaton, G, Stanford. 166, Rich Miano, DB, Hawaii. 208, Matt Monger, LB, Oklahoma State. 235, Mike Waters, RB, San Diego State. 262, Kerry Glenn, DB, Minnesota. 292, Brad White, DE, Texas Tech. 319, Bill Wallace, WR, Pittsburgh.

Philadelphia Eagles

9, Kevin Allen, T, Indiana. 37, Randall Cunningham, QB, Nevada-Las Vegas. 93, Greg Naron, G, North

Carolina. 121, Duane Jiles, LB, Texas Tech. 156, Ken Reeves, T, Texas A&M. 205, Tom Polley, LB, Nevada-Las Vegas. 231, Dave Toub, C, Texas-El Paso. 233, Joe Drake, DT, Arizona. 261, Mark Kelso, DB, William & Mary. 289, Herman Hunter, RB, Tennessee State. 317, Todd Russell, DB, Boston College.

Pittsburgh Steelers

20, Darryl Sims, DE, Wisconsin. 47, Mark Behning, T, Nebraska. 74, Liffort Hobley, DB, LSU. 101, Dan Turk, C, Wisconsin. 136, Cam Jacobs, LB, Kentucky. 160, Greg Carr, LB, Auburn. 187, Alan Andrews, TE, Rutgers. 214, Harry Newsome, P, Wake Forest. 241, Fred Small, LB, Washington. 242, Andre Harris, DB, Minnesota. 268, Oliver White, TE, Kentucky. 300, Terry Matichak, DB, Missouri. 327, Jeff Sanchez, DB, Georgia.

St. Louis Cardinals

18, Freddie Nunn, LB, Mississippi. 51, Scott Bergold, DT, Wisconsin. 72, Lance Smith, T, LSU. 104, Ron Wolfley, RB, West Virginia. 116, K.D. Dunn, TE, Clemson. 131, Louis Wong, G, Brigham Young. 158, Jay Novacek, WR, Wyoming. 212, Rob Monaco, G, Vanderbilt. 244, Scott Williams, TE, Georgia. 271, Dennis Williams, RB, Furman. 298, Ricky Anderson, K, Vanderbilt. 325, Lonnie Young, DB, Michigan State.

San Diego Chargers

12, Jim Lachey, G, Ohio State. 39, Wayne Davis, DB, Indiana State. 55, Jeff Dale, DB, LSU. 69, John Hendy, DB, Long Beach State. 96, Ralf Mojsiejenko, K-P, Michigan State. 150, Terry Lewis, DB, Michigan State. 196, Mark Fellows, LB, Montana State. 207, Curtis Adams, RB, Central Michigan. 234, Paul Berner, QB, Pacific. 252, Dan Remsberg, T, Abilene Christian. 264, David King, DB, Auburn. 291, Jeff Smith, DT, Kentucky. 318, Tony Simmons, DE, Tennessee. 329, Bret Pearson, TE, Wisconsin.

San Francisco 49ers
16, Jerry Rice, WR, Mississippi Valley. 75, Ricky Moore, RB, Alabama. 140, Bruce Collie, T, Texas-Arlington. 168, Scott Barry, QB, Cal-Davis. 308, David Wood, DE, Arizona. 336, Donald Chumley, DT, Georgia.

Seattle Seahawks
53, Owen Gill, RB, Iowa. 81, Danny Greene, WR, Washington. 109, Tony Davis, TE, Missouri. 123, Mark Napolitan, C, Michigan State. 128, Arnold Brown, DB, North Carolina Central. 137, Johnnie Jones, RB, Tennessee. 193, Ron Mattes, T, Virginia. 221, Judious Lewis, WR, Arkansas State. 248, Bob Otto, DE, Idaho State. 277, John Connor, QB, Arizona. 280, James Bowers, DB, Memphis State. 305, Louis Cooper, LB, Western Carolina.

Tampa Bay Buccaneers
8, Ron Holmes, DE, Washington. 64, Ervin Randle, LB, Baylor. 92, Mike Heaven, DB, Illinois. 176, Mike Prior, DB, Illinois State. 204, Phil Freeman, WR, Arizona. 232, Steve Calabria, QB, Colgate. 260, Donald Igwebuike, K, Clemson. 288, James Williams, RB, Memphis State. 316, Jim Rockford, DB, Oklahoma. 330, Jim Melka, LB, Wisconsin.

Washington Redskins
33, Tory Nixon, DB, San Diego State. 122, Raphel Cherry, QB, Hawaii. 163, Danzell Lee, TE, Lamar. 177, Jamie Harris, KR, Oklahoma State. 185, Lionel Vital, RB, Nicholis State. 219, Barry Wilburn, DB, Mississippi. 247, Mitch Geier, G, Troy State. 263, Terry Orr, RB, Texas. 290, Raleigh McKenzie, G, Tennessee. 304, Garry Kimble, DB, Sam Houston State. 309, Dean Hamel, DT, Tulsa. 331, Bryant Winn, LB, Houston.

1984
Statistics

Leading Rushers	Att.	Yards	Avg.	Long	TDs
AFC					
Jackson, Earnest, S.D.	296	1179	4.0	32	8
Allen, Marcus, L.A.	275	1168	4.2	52	13
Winder, Sammy, Den.	296	1153	3.9	24	4
Bell, Greg, Buff.	262	1100	4.2	85	7
McNeil, Freeman, N.Y.	229	1070	4.7	53	5
Pollard, Frank, Pitt.	213	851	4.0	52	6
James, Craig, N.E.	160	790	4.9	73	1
Moriarty, Larry, Hou.	189	785	4.2	51	6
McMillan, Randy, Ind.	163	705	4.3	31	5
Heard, Herman, K.C.	165	684	4.1	69	4
Green, Boyce, Clev.	202	673	3.3	29	0
Kinnebrew, Larry, Cin.	154	623	4.0	23	9
Abercrombie, Walter, Pitt.	145	610	4.2	31	1
Bennett, Woody, Mia.	144	606	4.2	23	7
Nathan, Tony, Mia.	118	558	4.7	22	1
Tatupu, Mosi, N.E.	133	553	4.2	20	4
Collins, Anthony, N.E.	138	550	4.0	21	5
Hector, Johnny, N.Y.	124	531	4.3	64	1
Dickey, Curtis, Ind.	131	523	4.0	30	3
Pruitt, Mike, Clev.	163	506	3.1	14	6
Carter, Joe, Mia.	100	495	5.0	35	1
Alexander, Charles, Cin.	132	479	3.6	22	2
NFC					
Dickerson, Eric, Rams	379	2105	5.6	66	14
Payton, Walter, Chi.	381	1684	4.4	72	11
Wilder, James, T.B.	407	1544	3.8	37	13
Riggs, Gerald, Atl.	353	1486	4.2	57	13
Tyler, Wendell, S.F.	246	1262	5.1	40	7
Riggins, John, Wash.	327	1239	3.8	24	14
Dorsett, Tony, Dall.	302	1189	3.9	31	6

95

Leading Rushers	Att.	Yards	Avg.	Long	TDs
Anderson, Ottis, St.L.	289	1174	4.1	24	6
Rogers, George, N.O.	239	914	3.8	28	2
Carpenter, Rob, N.Y.	250	795	3.2	22	7
Montgomery, Wilbert, Phil.	201	789	3.9	27	2
Anderson, Alfred, Minn.	201	773	3.8	23	2
Sims, Billy, Det.	130	687	5.3	81	5
Craig, Roger, S.F.	155	649	4.2	28	7
Gajan, Hokie, N.O.	102	615	6.0	62	5
Ellis, Gerry, G.B	123	581	4.7	50	4
Ivery, Eddie Lee, G.B.	99	552	5.6	49	6
Jones, James, Det.	137	532	3.9	34	3
Morris, Joe, N.Y.	133	510	3.8	28	4
Campbell, Earl, Hou.-N.O.	146	468	3.2	22	4
Brown, Ted, Minn.	98	442	4.5	19	3
Mitchell, Stump, St.L.	81	434	5.4	39	9

Lead Passers	Att.	Comp	Yds. Gnd.	TD Pass	Int.	Rating
AFC						
Marino, Dan, Mia.	564	362	5084	48	17	108.9
Eason, Tony, N.E.	431	259	3228	23	8	93.4
Fouts, Dan, S.D.	507	317	3740	19	17	83.4
Krieg, Dave, Sea.	480	276	3671	32	24	83.3
Anderson, Ken, Cin.	275	175	2107	10	12	81.0
Kenney, Bill, K.C.	282	151	2098	15	10	80.7
Moon, Warren, Hou.	450	259	3338	12	14	76.9
Elway, John, Den.	380	214	2598	18	15	76.8
Malone, Mark, Pitt.	272	147	2137	16	17	73.4
Ryan, Pat, N.Y.	285	156	1939	14	14	72.0
Wilson, Marc, L.A.	282	153	2151	15	17	71.7
McDonald, Paul, Clev.	493	271	3472	14	23	67.3
Ferguson, Joe, Buff.	344	191	1991	12	17	63.5
Blackledge, Todd, K.C.	294	147	1707	6	11	59.2
NFC						
Montana, Joe, S.F.	432	279	3630	28	10	102.9
Lomax, Neil, St.L.	560	345	4614	28	16	92.5

Lead Passers	Att.	Comp	Yds. Gnd.	TD Pass	Int.	Rat- ing
Bartkowski, Steve, Atl.	269	181	2158	11	10	89.7
Theismann, Joe, Wash.	477	283	3391	24	13	86.6
Dickey, Lynn, G.B.	401	237	3195	25	19	85.6
Danielson, Gary, Det.	410	252	3076	17	15	83.1
DeBerg, Steve, T.B.	509	308	3554	19	18	79.3
Kemp, Jeff, L.A.	284	143	2021	13	7	78.7
Simms, Phil, N.Y.	533	286	4044	22	18	78.1
Jaworski, Ron, Phil.	427	234	2754	16	14	73.5
White, Danny, Dall.	233	126	1580	11	11	71.5
Kramer, Tommy, Minn.	236	124	1678	9	10	70.6
Hogeboom, Gary, Dall.	367	195	2366	7	14	63.7
Todd, Richard, N.O.	312	161	2178	11	19	60.6

Leading Receivers	No.	Yards	Avg.	TDs
AFC				
Newsome, Ozzie, Clev.	89	1001	11.2	5
Stallworth, John, Pitt.	80	1395	17.4	11
Christensen, Todd, L.A.	80	1007	12.6	7
Largent, Steve, Sea.	74	1164	15.7	12
Clayton, Mark, Mia.	73	1389	19.0	18
Duper, Mark, Mia.	71	1306	18.4	8
Watson, Steve, Den.	69	1170	17.0	7
Smith, Tim, Hou.	69	1141	16.5	4
Franklin, Byron, Buff.	69	862	12.5	4
Shuler, Mickey, N.Y.	68	782	11.5	6
Ramsey, Derrick, N.E.	66	792	12.0	7
Collinsworth, Cris, Cin.	64	989	15.5	6
Allen, Marcus, L.A.	64	758	11.8	5
Marshall, Henry, K.C.	62	912	14.7	4
Joiner, Charlie, S.D.	61	793	13.0	6
Nathan, Tony, Mia.	61	579	9.5	2
Carson, Carlos, K.C.	57	1078	18.9	4
Holohan, Pete, S.D.	56	734	13.1	1
Winslow, Kellen, S.D.	55	663	12.1	2
Chandler, Wes, S.D.	52	708	13.6	6

Leading Receivers	No.	Yards	Avg.	TDs
NFC				
Monk, Art, Wash.	106	1372	12.9	7
Wilder, James, T.B.	85	685	8.1	0
Green, Roy, St.L.	78	1555	19.9	12
Jones, James, Det.	77	662	8.6	5
House, Kevin, T.B.	76	1005	13.2	5
Craig, Roger, S.F.	71	675	9.5	3
Anderson, Ottis, St.L.	70	611	8.7	2
Bailey, Stacey, Atl.	67	1138	17.0	6
Spagnola, John, Phil.	65	701	10.8	1
Lofton, James, G.B.	62	1361	22.0	7
Quick, Mike, Phil.	61	1052	17.2	9
Carter, Gerald, T.B.	60	816	13.6	5
Cosbie, Doug, Dall.	60	789	13.2	4
Montgomery, Wilbert, Phil.	60	501	8.4	0
Hill, Tony, Dall.	58	864	14.9	5
Clark, Dwight, S.F.	52	880	16.9	6
Tilley, Pat, St.L.	52	758	14.6	5
Jackson, Alfred, Atl.	52	731	14.1	2

Leading Interceptors	No.	Yards	Long	TDs
AFC				
Easley, Ken, Sea.	10	126	58	2
Brown, Dave, Sea.	8	179	90	2
Cherry, Deron, K.C.	7	140	67	0
Shell, Donnie, Pitt.	7	61	52	1
Haynes, Mike, L.A.	6	220	97	1
Blackwood, Glenn, Mia	6	169	50	0
Washington, Sam, Pitt.	6	138	69	2
NFC				
Flynn, Tom, G.B.	9	106	31	0
Lewis, Tim, G.B.	7	151	99	1
Downs, Mike, Dall.	7	126	27	1
Ellis, Ray, Phil.	7	119	31	0
Dean, Vernon, Wash.	7	114	36	2
Haynes, Mark, N.Y.	7	90	22	0

Leading Scorers, Kicking	PAT	FG	TP
AFC			
Anderson, Gary, Pitt.	45-45	24-32	117
Johnson, Norm, Sea.	50-51	20-24	110
Franklin, Tony, N.E.	42-42	22-28	108
Lowery, Nick, K.C.	35-35	23-33	104
Breech, Jim, Cin.	37-37	22-31	103
Karlis, Rich, Den.	38-41	21-28	101
Bahr, Chris, L.A.	40-42	20-27	100
Bahr, Matt, Clev.	25-25	24-32	97
Von Schamann, Uwe, Mia.	66-70	9-19	93
Benirschke, Rolf, S.D	41-41	17-26	92
NFC			
Wersching, Ray, S.F.	56-56	25-35	131
Moseley, Mark, Wash.	48-51	24-31	120
O'Donoghue, Neil, St.L.	48-51	23-35	117
McFadden, Paul, Phil.	26-27	30-37	116
Lansford, Mike, L.A.	37-38	25-33	112
Septien, Rafael, Dall.	33-34	23-29	102
Thomas, Bob, Chi.	35-37	22-28	101
Ariri, Obed, T.B.	38-40	19-26	95
Andersen, Morten, N.O.	34-34	20-27	94
Luckhurst, Mick, Atl.	31-31	20-27	91

Leading Scorers, Touchdowns	TDs	Rush	Rec.	Ret.	TP
AFC					
Allen, Marcus, L.A.	18	13	5	0	108
Clayton, Mark, Mia.	18	0	18	0	108
Johnson, Pete, S.D.-Mia.	12	12	0	0	72
Largent, Steve, Sea.	12	0	12	0	72
Lipps, Louis, Pitt.	11	1	9	1	66
Stallworth, John, Pitt.	11	0	11	0	66
Kinnebrew, Larry, Cin.	10	9	1	0	60
Turner, Daryl, Sea.	10	0	10	0	60
Jackson, Earnest, S.D.	9	8	1	0	54
Bell, Greg, Buff.	8	7	1	0	48
Bennett, Woody, Mia.	8	7	1	0	48

Leading Scorers, Touchdowns	TDs	Rush	Rec.	Ret.	TP
Duper, Mark, Mia.	8	0	8	0	48
Paige, Tony, N.Y.	8	7	1	0	48
Christensen, Todd, L.A.	7	0	7	0	42
Dennard, Preston, Buff.	7	0	7	0	42
NFC					
Dickerson, Eric, L.A.	14	14	0	0	84
Riggins, John, Wash.	14	14	0	0	84
Riggs, Gerald, Atl.	13	13	0	0	78
Wilder, James, T.B.	13	13	0	0	78
Green, Roy, St.L.	12	0	12	0	72
Mitchell, Stump, St.L.	11	9	2	0	66
Payton, Walter, Chi.	11	11	0	0	66
Solomon, Freddie, S.F.	11	1	10	0	66
Craig, Roger, S.F.	10	7	3	0	60
Coffman, Paul, G.B.	9	0	9	0	54
Quick, Mike, Phil.	9	0	9	0	54
Tyler, Wendell, S.F.	9	7	2	0	54
Anderson, Ottis, St.L.	8	6	2	0	48
Carpenter, Rob, N.Y.	8	7	1	0	48
Ellard, Henry, L.A.	8	0	6	2	48

Leading Punters	No.	Yards	Long	Avg.
AFC				
Arnold, Jim, K.C.	98	4397	63	44.9
Roby, Reggie, Mia.	51	2281	69	44.7
Stark, Rohn, Ind.	98	4383	72	44.7
Cox, Steve, Clev.	74	3213	69	43.4
Prestridge, Luke, N.E.	44	1884	89	42.8
McInally, Pat, Cin.	67	2832	61	42.3
Camarillo, Rich, N.E.	48	2020	61	42.1
Buford, Maury, S.D.	66	2773	60	42.0
Kidd, John, Buff.	88	3696	63	42.0
Guy, Ray, L.A.	91	3809	63	41.9
Colquitt, Craig, Pitt.	70	2883	62	41.2
Norman, Chris, Den.	96	3850	83	40.1
Ramsey, Chuck, N.Y.	74	2935	64	39.7

Leading Punters	No.	Yards	Long	Avg.
NFC				
Hansen, Brian, N.O.	69	3020	66	43.8
Coleman, Greg, Minn.	82	3473	62	42.4
Scribner, Bucky, G.B.	85	3596	61	42.3
Horan, Mike, Phil.	92	3880	69	42.2
Giacomarro, Ralph, Atl.	68	2855	58	42.0
Garcia, Frank, T.B.	68	2849	60	41.9
Runager, Max, S.F.	56	2341	59	41.8
Black, Mike, Det.	76	3164	63	41.6
Finzer, David, Chi.	83	3328	87	40.1
Jennings, Dave, N.Y.	90	3598	54	40.0
Hayes, Jeff, Wash.	72	2834	59	39.4

Leading Punt Returners	No.	Yards	Avg.	TDs
AFC				
Martin, Mike, Cin.	24	376	15.7	0
Lipps, Louis, Pitt.	53	656	12.4	1
Willhite, Gerald, Den.	20	200	10.0	0
Fryar, Irving, N.E.	36	347	9.6	0
Wilson, Don, Buff.	33	297	9.0	1
Pruitt, Greg, L.A.	53	473	8.9	0
Springs, Kirk, N.Y.	28	247	8.8	0
Smith, J.T., K.C.	39	332	8.5	0
Walker, Fulton, Mia.	21	169	8.0	0
Brennan, Brian, Clev.	25	199	8.0	0
NFC				
Ellard, Henry, L.A.	30	403	13.4	2
McLemore, Dana, S.F.	45	521	11.6	1
Mitchell, Stump, St.L.	38	333	8.8	0
Fields, Jitter, N.O.	27	236	8.7	0
Nelms, Mike, Wash.	49	428	8.7	0
Fisher, Jeff, Chi.	57	492	8.6	0
Martin, Robbie, Det.	25	210	8.4	0
Allen, Gary, Dall.	54	446	8.3	0
Nelson, Darrin, Minn.	23	180	7.8	0
Bright, Leon, T.B	23	173	7.5	0

Leading Kickoff Returners	No.	Yards	Avg.	TDs
AFC				
Humphery, Bobby, N.Y.	22	675	30.7	1
Williams, Dokie, L.A.	24	621	25.9	0
Anderson, Larry, Ind.	22	525	23.9	0
Springs, Kirk, N.Y.	23	521	22.7	0
Roaches, Carl, Hou.	30	679	22.6	0
James, Lionel, S.D.	43	959	22.3	0
Collins, Anthony, N.E.	25	544	21.8	0
Montgomery, Cleotha, L.A.	26	555	21.3	0
Walker, Fulton, Mia.	29	617	21.3	0
Williams, Van, Buff.	39	820	21.0	0
Jennings, Stanford, Cin.	22	452	20.5	0
Erenberg, Rich, Pitt.	28	575	20.5	0
Smith, Phil, Ind.	32	651	20.3	1
Paige, Stephon, K.C.	27	544	20.1	0
Williams, Jon, N.E.	23	461	20.0	0
NFC				
Redden, Barry, L.A.	23	530	23.0	0
Mitchell, Stump, St.L.	35	804	23.0	0
Nelson, Darrin, Minn.	39	891	22.8	0
Anthony, Tyrone, N.O.	22	490	22.3	0
Morton, Michael, T.B.	38	835	22.0	0
Rodgers, Del, G.B.	39	843	21.6	1
Anderson, Alfred, Minn.	30	639	21.3	0
Hill, Drew, L.A.	26	543	20.9	0
Monroe, Carl, S.F.	27	561	20.8	0
Nelms, Mike, Wash.	42	860	20.5	0
Allen, Gary, Dall.	33	666	20.2	0
McSwain, Chuck, Dall.	20	403	20.2	0
Hayes, Joe, Phil.	22	44	20.0	0
Duckett, Kenny, N.O.	29	580	20.0	0
McConkey, Phil, N.Y.	28	541	19.3	0

1985
NFL Schedule

Sunday, September 8
Denver at L.A. Rams
Detroit at Atlanta
Green Bay at New England
Indianapolis at Pittsburgh
Kan. City at New Orleans
Miami at Houston
N.Y. Jets at L.A. Raiders
Philadelphia at N.Y. Giants
St. Louis at Cleveland
San Diego at Buffalo
San Fran. at Minnesota
Seattle at Cincinnati
Tampa Bay at Chicago

Monday, September 9
Washington at Dallas

Thursday, September 12
L.A. Raiders at Kansas City

Sunday, September 15
Atlanta at San Francisco
Buffalo at N.Y. Jets
Cincinnati at St. Louis
Dallas at Detroit
Houston at Washington
Indianapolis at Miami
L.A. Rams at Philadelphia
Minnesota at Tampa Bay
New England at Chicago
New Orleans at Denver
N.Y. Giants at Green Bay
Seattle at San Diego

Monday, September 16
Pittsburgh at Cleveland

Thursday, September 19
Chicago at Minnesota

Sunday, September 22
Cleveland at Dallas
Denver at Atlanta
Detroit at Indianapolis
Houston at Pittsburgh
Kansas City at Miami
New England at Buffalo
N.Y. Jets vs. Green Bay
  at Milwaukee
Phil. at Washington
St. Louis at N.Y. Giants
San Diego at Cincinnati
San Fran. at L.A. Raiders
Tampa Bay at New Orleans

Monday, September 23
L.A. Rams at Seattle

Sunday, September 29
Atlanta at L.A. Rams
Cleveland at San Diego
Dallas at Houston
Green Bay at St. Louis
Indianapolis at N.Y. Jets
L.A. Raiders at New Eng.
Miami at Denver
Minnesota at Buffalo
New Orleans at San Fran.

N.Y. Giants at Phil.
Seattle at Kansas City
Tampa Bay at Detroit
Washington at Chicago

Monday, September 30
Cincinnati at Pittsburgh

Sunday, October 6
Buffalo at Indianapolis
Chicago at Tampa Bay
Dallas at N.Y. Giants
Detroit at Green Bay
Houston at Denver
Kansas City at L.A. Raiders
Minnesota at L.A. Rams
New England at Cleveland
N.Y. Jets at Cincinnati
Phil. at New Orleans
Pittsburgh at Miami
San Diego at Seattle
San Francisco at Atlanta

Monday, October 7
St. Louis at Washington

Sunday, October 13
Atlanta at Seattle
Buffalo at New England
Chicago at San Francisco
Cleveland at Houston
Denver at Indianapolis
Detroit at Washington
Kansas City at San Diego
L.A. Rams at Tampa Bay
Minnesota vs. Green Bay
    at Milwaukee
New Orl. at L.A. Raiders
N.Y. Giants at Cincinnati
Philadelphia at St. Louis
Pittsburgh at Dallas

Monday, October 14
Miami at N.Y. Jets

Sunday, October 20
Cincinnati at Houston
Dallas at Philadelphia
Indianapolis at Buffalo
L.A. Raiders at Cleveland
L.A. Rams at Kansas City
New Orleans at Atlanta
N.Y. Jets at New England
St. Louis at Pittsburgh
San Diego at Minnesota
San Francisco at Detroit
Seattle at Denver
Tampa Bay at Miami
Washington at N.Y. Giants

Monday, October 21
Green Bay at Chicago

Sunday, October 27
Atlanta at Dallas
Buffalo at Philadelphia
Denver at Kansas City
Green Bay at Indianap.
Houston at St. Louis
Miami at Detroit
Minnesota at Chicago
New England at Tampa Bay
N.Y. Giants at New Orl.
Pittsburgh at Cincinnati
San Fran. at L.A. Rams
Seattle at N.Y. Jets
Washington at Cleveland

Monday, October 28
San Diego at L.A. Raiders

Sunday, November 3
Chicago at Green Bay
Cincinnati at Buffalo

Cleveland at Pittsburgh
Denver at San Diego
Detroit at Minnesota
Kansas City at Houston
L.A. Raiders at Seattle
Miami at New England
New Orleans at L.A. Rams
N.Y. Jets at Indianapolis
Philadelphia at San Fran.
Tampa Bay at N.Y. Giants
Washington at Atlanta

Monday, November 4
Dallas at St. Louis

Sunday, November 10
Atlanta at Philadelphia
Cleveland at Cincinnati
Dallas at Washington
Detroit at Chicago
Green Bay at Minnesota
Houston at Buffalo
Indianapolis at New Engl.
L.A. Raiders at San Diego
L.A. Rams at N.Y. Giants
N.Y. Jets at Miami
Pittsburgh at Kansas City
St. Louis at Tampa Bay
Seattle at New Orleans

Monday, November 11
San Francisco at Denver

Sunday, November 17
Buffalo at Cleveland
Chicago at Dallas
Cincinnati at L.A. Raiders
Kansas City at San Fran.
L.A. Rams at Atlanta
Miami at Indianapolis
Minnesota at Detroit
New England at Seattle

New Orleans vs. Green Bay
  at Milwaukee
Pittsburgh at Houston
St. Louis at Philadelphia
San Diego at Denver
Tampa Bay at N.Y. Jets

Monday, November 18
N.Y. Giants at Washington

Sunday, November 24
Atlanta at Chicago
Cincinnati at Cleveland
Denver at L.A. Raiders
Detroit at Tampa Bay
Green Bay at L.A. Rams
Indianapolis at Kan. City
Miami at Buffalo
New England at N.Y. Jets
New Orleans at Minnesota
N.Y. Giants at St. Louis
Philadelphia at Dallas
San Diego at Houston
Washington at Pittsburgh

Monday, November 25
Seattle at San Francisco

Thursday, November 28
N.Y. Jets at Detroit
St. Louis at Dallas

Sunday, December 1
Buffalo at San Diego
Cleveland at N.Y. Giants
Denver at Pittsburgh
Houston at Cincinnati
Kansas City at Seattle
L.A. Raiders at Atlanta
L.A. Rams at New Orleans
Minnesota at Philadelphia
New Engl. at Indianapolis

San Fran. at Washington
Tampa Bay at Green Bay

Monday, December 2
Chicago at Miami

Thursday, December 5
Pittsburgh at San Diego

Sunday, December 8
Atlanta at Kansas City
Cleveland at Seattle
Dallas at Cincinnati
Detroit at New England
Indianapolis at Chicago
L.A. Raiders at Denver
Miami at Green Bay
New Orleans at St. Louis
N.Y. Giants at Houston
N.Y. Jets at Buffalo
Tampa Bay at Minnesota
Washington at Phil.

Monday, December 9
L.A. Rams at San Fran.

Saturday, December 14
Chicago at N.Y. Jets
Kansas City at Denver

Sunday, December 15
Buffalo at Pittsburgh
Cincinnati at Washington
Green Bay at Detroit

Houston at Cleveland
Indianap. at Tampa Bay
Minnesota at Atlanta
N.Y. Giants at Dallas
Phil. at San Diego
St. Louis at L.A. Rams
San Fran. at New Orleans
Seattle at L.A. Raiders

Monday, December 16
New England at Miami

Friday, December 20
Denver at Seattle

Saturday, December 21
Pittsburgh at N.Y. Giants
Washington at St. Louis

Sunday, December 22
Atlanta at New Orleans
Buffalo at Miami
Chicago at Detroit
Cincinnati at New England
Cleveland at N.Y. Jets
Dallas at San Francisco
Green Bay at Tampa Bay
Houston at Indianapolis
Philadelphia at Minnesota
San Diego at Kansas City

Monday, December 23
L.A. Raiders at L.A. Rams

BRUCE WEBER PICKS
HOW THEY'LL FINISH IN 1985

AFC East

1. Miami
2. New York
3. New England
4. Buffalo
5. Indianapolis

AFC Central

1. Cincinnati
2. Pittsburgh
3. Houston
4. Cleveland

AFC West

1. Seattle
2. Los Angeles
3. Denver
4. Kansas City
5. San Diego

NFC East

1. St. Louis
2. Washington
3. New York
4. Dallas
5. Philadelphia

NFC Central

1. Chicago
2. Tampa Bay
3. Detroit
4. Green Bay
5. Minnesota

NFC West

1. San Francisco
2. Los Angeles
3. Atlanta
4. New Orleans

AFC Champions: Miami
NFC Champions: Chicago
Super Bowl Champions: Miami

YOU PICK
HOW THEY'LL FINISH IN 1985

AFC East

1. Dolphins
2. Jets
3. Patriots
4. Bills
5. Colts

AFC Central

1. Steelers
2. Bengals
3. Browns
4. Oilers

AFC West

1. Raiders
2. Broncos
3. Seahawks
4. Chargers
5. Chiefs

NFC East

1. Cowboys
2. Cardinals
3. Redskins
4. Giants
5. Eagles

NFC Central

1. Bears
2. Lions
3. Buccaneers
4. Packers
5. Vikings

NFC West

1. 49ers
2. Rams
3. Saints
4. Falcons

AFC Champions: Pittsburgh Steelers
NFC Champions: San Francisco 49ers
Super Bowl Champions: San Francisco 49ers